Insights for
Believers

Discerning Your Journey

Enoch Elijah

Trilogy Christian Publishers
A Wholly Owned Subsidary of Trinity Broadcasting Network
2442 Michelle Drive
Tustin, CA 92780

Scriptures are taken from the King James Version of the
Bible.
For information, address Trilogy Christian Publishing
Rights Department, 2442 Michelle Drive, Tustin, Ca 92780.
Trilogy Christian Publishing/ TBN and colophon are trade-
marks of Trinity Broadcasting Network.
For information about special discounts for bulk purchases,
please contact Trilogy Christian Publishing.
Manufactured in the United States of America

Trilogy Disclaimer: The views and content expressed in this
book are those of the author and may not necessarily reflect
the views and doctrine of Trilogy Christian Publishing or the
Trinity Broadcasting Network.

Cover photo credit: John Towner (via Unsplash.com)

10 9 8 7 6 5 4 3 2 1
Library of Congress Cataloging-in-Publication Data is avail-
able.
ISBN 978-1-64088-499-1
ISBN 978-1-64088-500-4

This book is dedicated to every Believer in Christ Jesus our Lord, with the hope it helps and enables them to navigate through the seasons of their development in Christ.

"Whoso keepth the commandment shall feel no evil thing: and a wise man's heart discerneth both time and judgment."

(Ecclesiastes 8:5)

Discernment is recognition of facts by observation or reflection during specific periods of time or seasons in our lives. After discerning the facts during a period of time in our life, we must determine based on those facts if we are moving forward in our development in Christ.

TABLE OF CONTENTS

INTRODUCTION

Blessed be the name of God for ever and ever, for wisdom and might are His. And he changes times and seasons; He removes kings and set up kings; He gives wisdom unto the wise; and knowledge to them that know understanding.

(Daniel 2:20–21)

The intent of this work is to communicate to Believers, the need to gain an accurate and deep intuitive understanding of their journey as a Believer in Christ. As Daniel states, "God gives wisdom unto the wise and knowledge to them that know understanding."

God sets up time and periods to support appointed occasions in our lives.

How do we recognize the indicators (good or bad) of our journey and how to follow the order of things God has set before us? God will reveal to you the paths to dwell in and show you the impacts the leaders of the world have as you gain knowledge of Him, then you will know understanding. How does this relate to God's purpose for those who believe?

To know God's purpose for the Believer, you must understand the changing of the season in your life that has been established (set in place), which communicates to your position in Christ. Are you able to discern where you are in your spiritual walk and the true possibilities available in Christ?

The principle thing is to seek God for wisdom to gain understanding of how to progress in our new-found life.

God's people are hindered from obtaining the benefits of a new life because of a lack of knowledge; we lack knowledge because we fail to study God's Word and at times, and we reject the knowledge provided from God through His Word and commandments.

When we learn to fear and reverence the Lord, through seeking His will, then we will be able to render a verdict of what period of time we are in, relating to the history and destiny of man as laid out in the Bible and the season of time in our individual lives we are in relating to our growth and relationship to God through Christ.

Yea, if thou criest after knowledge, and liftest up thy voice for understanding;
If thou seek her as silver, and searchest for her as for hid treasures;
Then shalt thou understand the fear of the Lord, and find the knowledge of God.
For the Lord giveth wisdom: out of his mouth cometh knowledge and understanding.
He layeth up sound wisdom for the righteous: he is a buckler to them that walk uprightly.
He keepeth the paths of judgment, and preserveth the way of his saints.
Then shalt thou understand righteousness, and judgment, and equity; yea, every good path.
(Proverbs 2:3–9)

I invite you to read all the scriptures referenced in this work. It will give you a greater insight into the thoughts relating to what you read and most of all it gives the Holy Ghost the chance to work as it interacts with the inner man by the Spirit of God.

PROLOGUE

Our basic premise for this work is formed from the temptation of Jesus after being led of the Spirit into the wilderness to be tempted of the devil.

Then was Jesus led up of the spirit into the wilderness to be tempted of the devil. And when he had fasted forty days and forty nights, he was afterward a hungered.
(Matthew 4:1–2)

This illustrates the battle to understand the influence of temptation in our lives and the possibility of falling to the wiles of temptation and erroneous beliefs.

A reoccurring theme in the life of a Believer is this cycle of test, decision, then result, revealed in the devil's temptation of Jesus.

Our goal is to discuss a few key insights to help Believers as they progress along the journey of becoming a new creature in Christ.

Understand Jesus had just been baptized and beginning His walk in the call for His life. Just as we after accepting Christ began our walk.

I pray the majority of the results from your decisions line up with God's will as you move through the different phases of your growth process.

The ministry of Christ begins in Matthew 3:16. Luke gives more detail of the baptism; he said, "The Holy Ghost descended in a bodily shape like a dove upon Jesus" (Luke 3:22). Filling and covering every part of Christ mind, body, and soul. Just as Jesus begun His ministry and then fulfilling His destiny upon the cross. How do we determine what is our destiny? Has the Holy Ghost descended on you as in Acts 2:1–4? What is your relationship with God right now? Do you know what season of our life you are in and how are the current spiritual influences impacting you?

Consider each insight presented in this writing; does it provide a true representation of where you are along the road of your development and destiny?

The whole life experience is a form of a test developing us for entrance into the kingdom to come. Israel's experiences in the Old Testament is an illustration of this for the Believer's journey of today.

The Bible is a puzzle waiting for us to put the pieces together. It is amazing how God orchestrates the events of the "Bible" into a maze-like structure where everything ends up as it should at the expected end.

Jesus Fasted Forty Days!

The number 40 is significant in the numerology of the Bible. The number 40 is mentioned 146 times in scripture, the number 40 generally symbolizes a period of testing, trial, or probation. During Moses's life he lived forty years in Egypt and forty years in the desert; each 40 years were seasons of development before he knew God had selected him to lead his people out of slavery.

After Israel exited Egypt they found the promise land and searched it for forty days (Numbers 13:25), their faith failed at the entrance to possessing the promise (Numbers 13:31), which resulted in probation for Israel due to a lack of faith, causing them to wonder in the wilderness for forty years (Numbers 14:22–34).

Don't be a wonderer in your walk with God, seek Him for guidance that He may reveal and plainly show the paths for you to dwell in!

Thus saith the Lord, Stand ye in the ways, and see, and ask for the old paths, where is the good way, and walk therein, and ye shall find rest for your souls. But they said, we will not walk therein.

(Jeremiah 6:16)

INSIGHT #1

ORIGINATED IN GOD

The number "1" marks the beginning.
Our beginning and origin were in God before life began in this current world.

Before I formed thee in the belly, I knew thee, and before thou camest forth out of the womb I sanctified thee, and I ordained thee a prophet unto the nations.
(Jeremiah 1:5)

Lord, thou hast been our dwelling place in all generations. Before the mountains were brought forth, or ever thou hadst formed the earth and the world, even from everlasting to everlasting, thou art God.
(Psalms 90:1–2)

These verses recognize that God is eternal and God knew us before we were born. He has always been a dwelling place (in all generations), with an inference of throughout eternity, meaning before this current world and after this current world when the new heaven and earth are revealed.

Think about the following concept:

In Genesis 1:26–27, God said, "Let us make man." He made male and female in these verses. Please observe it was not mentioned that these men and woman *had a living soul*. Where in Genesis 2:7 after the creation was finished God rested and then formed man (Adam) from the dust of the ground and God breathed the breath of life making him a living soul (eternal). Doesn't this sound like two separate creations of man?

In Genesis chapter 1 the making man was a plural connotation, being made in a broad sense, the widest application. The word *man* in the verse is speaking of mankind in a generic sense.

In Genesis chapter 2 man (Adam) was a specific and singular form. Like a potter does when making a vessel (Jeremiah 18:3–6). Man, in this verse, has specificity with eternal capability (the breath of God infused making him a living soul). Adam was different from the people made in Genesis chapter 1. Eve was not formed until Genesis 2:21–22.

Adam being formed on the seventh day in Eden (a paradise) is indicative and a foreshadow of the same process God will perform in the book of Revelations when the new heaven and earth, the New Jerusalem (our future Eden) will be established (Revelations 21:1–3).

I know the people in Genesis chapter 1 and Adam in chapter 2 are two different occurrences because of this question; where did the people come from in Genesis 4:13–16 that Cain was afraid of when God pushed him out from His presence for killing Able?

Since creation there has been two groups of people, those in God's presence (Adam) and those not in the presence of God (the men and women from Genesis chapter 1).

The issue today is no one wants to acknowledge there are people that aren't saved (a member of God's family). We are in a period of acceptance and tolerance.

Yet through Christ all men can be saved and gain eternal life. An abundant life now and eternal life at Christ's return.

Believest thou not that I am in the Father, and the Father in me? The words that I speak unto you I speak not of myself: but the Father that dwelleth in me, he doeth the works.

(John 14:10)

And I will pray the Father, and he will give you another Comforter (Holy Ghost), that he may abide with you forever;
Even the Spirit of truth; whom the world cannot receive, because it seeth him not, neither knoweth him: but ye know him; for he dwelleth with you, and shall be in you.

(John 14:16–17)

At that day (when Christ is resurrected and returns to the Father) ye shall know that I am in my Father, and ye in me, and I in you.

(John 14:20)

Belief in Christ provides the opportunity to be restored into the presence of God for all men.

Remember: "Christ was the firstborn of every creature; raised from the dead: and by Him was all things created, in heaven and earth, visible, invisible, dominions, principalities, and powers; all things being created by Him." (Colossians 1:16)

We must understand our life is not a spur of the

11

moment event when we were conceived by our parents. We were known prior to conception and we are known after conception as we dwell in this current life; waiting for the day of the physical reunion back into the presence of God. This truth is revealed through the journey of Israel.

It is interesting that Israel and the Believer's starting point with God is also the ending point. He (God) is from everlasting to everlasting; time past and time in the future, He is eternal.

Israel was in Canaan (Genesis 37:1) before their journey to Egypt. The same land that was given back to them after their exit from Egypt (a symbol of bondage and carnality of the world). The return to Canaan their promise land (Joshua 17:17–18) was not an overwhelming success. There were seven tribes' slack to receive their inheritance (Joshua 18:2–3).

The Believer's journey is not much different. We began in the heart of God before the world was framed, born into the world (carnality) and returned to the heart and family of God after His grace provided the way through belief in Christ Jesus. We too must fight and pray to obtain our inheritance as Israel did.

Why does God take Israel from freedom to bondage and then back to freedom? It is all about worship. The Lord desired for man to yield his service to Him (God) because man wanted to.

Life is our proving ground. As we overcome the entanglement of the world, we will be found worthy of everlasting life. The failure of Satan, Adam, and Eve caused separation from God starting a spiritual war. Hence God set in motion the reconciliation of man through Christ. Though we are born in sin due to Adam; we can believe our way back into the presence of God through Christ.

Look at the following types (a category of people or things having common characteristics) shown in the history of Israel (Old Testament) that translates to the New Testament Church and the Believer of today.

1) Pharaoh (Exodus 1:15–22) and Herod (Matthew 2:16–20) killing of Israel's young with a purpose to stop the destiny that had already been set by God through these births. Yet Moses and Jesus survived. Abortion stops children from entering the world that could make a great difference for the benefit of the kingdom of God (God knew us and had a plan for us before we were born).

2) Blood on the door post (Exodus 12:3–7 and crossing the sea (Exodus 14:8–31); Christ our Passover lamb (Matthew 26:2 and Matthew 27:37–58) and Baptism (Matthew 3:13–17, Acts 2:37–41)—we are baptized into Christ our Passover lamb and the family of God being delivered from sin and the world.

3) The quail and water from a rock (Exodus 16:12–15 and 17:3–7); God shows he is a provider; Matthew 6:25–26 and 1 Peter 5:7—God lets us know, not to worry we are valuable to Him and for us to cast all our cares on Him.

4) Replaced worship with idolatry—accepting and practicing beliefs of other forms of worship; allowing thoughts and ideas that are against the will of God (Exodus 32, Numbers 25, and Ezekiel 8:12–18); God opposes worship not directed toward Him because it causes the destruction of man's soul (Romans 1:19–32)—Tammuz (Ezekiel 8:14), Baal (1 Kings 16:31), and Ashtoreth (1 Kings 11:5); Judges 2:13, 2 Kings 23:13, and 1 Samuel 12:10; these forms of worship are still present in our religious beliefs today.

And fear not them which kill the body, but are not able to kill the soul; but rather fear him which is able to destroy both the soul and body in hell.

(Matthew 10:28)

Idolatry opens the avenue for the people of God to be hindered in every good work and puts them in danger of losing their soul.

Falsehood (errant religious practices) disrupts our relationship with God and our ability to operate in the fullness of spirit that He has provided.

We must think of life as God purposed it. It is the road to demonstrate our choice to unify with God, which is the avenue to eternity.

Just as Israel had to change their thought process to line up with God after the exit from Egypt; we must do the same.

I BESEECH you therefore, brethren, by the mercies of God, that ye present your bodies a living sacrifice, holy, acceptable unto God, which is your reasonable service.
And be not conformed to this world; but be ye transformed by the renewing of your mind, that ye may prove what is that good, and acceptable, and perfect, will of God.

(Romans 12:1–2)

Are you a Joshua or Caleb willing to take and possess what God gave you before the beginning of time (Numbers 14:6–9)?

Seeing therefore it remaineth that some must enter therein, and they to whom it was first preached entered

not in because of unbelief:
Again, he limiteth a certain day, saying in David, To-
day, after so long a time; as it is said, Today if ye will
hear his voice, harden not your hearts.
For if Jesus had given them rest, then would he not
afterward have spoken of another day.
There remaineth therefore a rest to the people of God.
For he that is entered into his rest, he also hath ceased
from his own works, as God did from his. (on the sev-
enth day)
Let us labour therefore to enter into that rest, lest any
man fall after the same example of unbelief.
(Hebrews 4:6–11)

God has set the choice before you of life and death or blessing and cursing (Deuteronomy 30:11–20).

Are you at the beginning of the revelation of Jesus Christ, your life being changed through Him? Has the knowledge that God is your father and you were known of Him before the beginning of time a realization for you? Do you understand He has always been aware of your life events past, present and future as you progress through the journey to become like Him?

You are a spiritual being created in the image of God. Make the transition from a natural thought process to a spiritual one.

The number "one" marks the beginning. Light was created on day one of creation.

Accepting Christ is your beginning and the point of us being enlighten by God. If you have accepted Him, you are now in route to obtain the promises of God.

Obtaining the original position, you had, in the mind of God before life begun in this current world.

Before I formed thee in the belly, I knew thee, and before thou camest forth out of the womb I sanctified thee, and I ordained thee a prophet unto the nations.

(Jeremiah 1:5)

THE JOURNEY

The number "2" shows there is a difference between good and evil.

The journey is the return of God's people from exile. Many times, in the Bible Israel were in situations that caused them to reflect and repent to obtain deliverance. The New Testament Church must also navigate its way out of the bondages the world presents; thereby experiencing the fullness of the testimony of Christ.

Through Christ, overcoming all opposition and hindrances entering into the life God has for us, experiencing living in the concepts of the kingdom of God in the fullness of the testimony of Christ.

Woe unto them that call evil good, and good evil; that put darkness for light, and light for darkness; that put better for sweet, and sweet for bitter!
Woe unto them that are wise in their own eyes, and prudent in their own sight!
                                                    (Isaiah 5:20–21)

Is this where we are today not able to discern good from evil? Are the same seducing spirits that deceived Eve to seduce Adam and that deceived Israel, now deceiving us? Yes!

We are in a culture where there is no wrong or right. This concept is even being taught in schools. The student's answers are relative based on their views and how they perceive the questions.

Our nation has entered a period of time where the rights of the people outweigh the laws of God. There is no righteousness or unrighteousness; it's all from the perspective of each person.

You should read the whole book of Isaiah it has sixty-six chapters just as the Bible has sixty-six books. It gives a picture of the journey of Israel during the time of Isaiah it provides an allegory (something that can be interpreted to reveal a hidden meaning) for the Believers journey of today. At the end of the book there are prophesies that are relevant to the end of time as we know it.

What are the far-reaching plans and impact of God in your life? Events happen for our benefit. Sometimes we make decisions that place us on a different road but God is able to get us to our destination.

Look at the specifics of Israel's journey (Genesis 37:1), they were already in Canaan, but a drought was coming; God allowed Joseph to be sold (what seems to be a detour—Genesis 37:16–28).

God was providing a way for His people to survive, while at the same time setting up a situation to illustrate the need for a return to God for our benefit today. Providing a prototype for the New Testament Church (sold in sin by Adams actions, but delivered by Christ and returned to God).

If we look at the sale of Joseph closer, we can see God working the maze of traveled paths meeting in one spot at a specific time to provide a glimpse of just how in control God is (because He Is: self-existing within

Himself). What are the events or interactions that has occurred in your life that are helping you find the path of your journey?

Jacob was the grandson of Abraham, making Joseph the great grandson of Abraham. He (Joseph) was sold to the descendants of his great uncles. Both the Ishmaelites and the Midianites were descendants from the sons of Abraham just as Joseph was.

Abraham's second wife Hagar was Sarai (Abraham's first wife) maid that was given to Abraham because she (Sarai) had not bare him any children (Genesis 16:3–11) and the name of Hagar's son was Ishmael (the Ishmaelites that bought Joseph).

Sarai Abraham's first wife bore him a son (Genesis 21:1–3) and his name was Isaac (Jacob's father/ Joseph grandfather).

Abraham's third wife (after Sarai's death) was Keturah and she bore him six sons (Genesis 25:1–2), and one of them was named Midian (the Midianites that bought Joseph).

This is amazing because Hagar left Egypt to follow and serve the patriarchs of God's people (Abraham and Sarah). Keturah is a form of the name Cassia (Psalms 45:8), which was one of the names of Job's daughters after Job was restored (Job 42:14). We'll talk about Job in "Insight No. 8" of this work.

This event (the sale of Joseph) can be linked all the way to today. Ishmael's descendants are the founders of Islam through Mohammed in Mecca (Saudi Arabia) and Midian's descendants lived east of Israel (Syria, Iraq, Iran). They are all relatives that are still at odds with each other until today. At odds because Muslims believe that the monotheistic (belief in one God; the God of Adam, Abraham, Isaac, and Jacob) was errored and Mohammad born in Mecca in 570 AD was raised up to get the nations of the world back to what they believe to be the true worship of God.

In the sale of Joseph to the Ishmaelites and Midianites, we have and allegory: God's people being sold into bondage yet delivered to take their rightful inheritance. Fleeing the world and offering a sweet smell of praise to the Father.

Joseph's experience was the key event showing the picture of Israel (God's natural people) traveling the path set up by the Lord, matching the plan for God's spiritual people (Believers) from the days of Adam to the days of Jesus. Adam was already in Eden (the promise), he gave up his right to reign through disobedience and failure to recognize the differences between good and evil presented by Satan, which sent him into exile from Eden. Jesus came to restore us to the promise and deliver us from bondage (Romans 5:12–21).

The Bible is the greatest book ever written, only if we take the time to put all the pieces of the puzzle together.

All through the Bible there are pictures that illustrate God's plans to bring man back to Him.

Think of the great flood (Genesis chapter 7); it rained and the flood was on the earth forty days. What were the sins of man at this time that brought the flood? It was the same mindset we have today, there is no right and wrong; evil is good and good is evil, and truth is how and what we perceive it to be.

To be friends with the world means you can't be a friend (son/daughter) of God. God's kingdom is not of the world nor is our fight a worldly fight (John 18:36).

Our journey is to relearn how to commune with

God and be led by the Holy Ghost.

Israel travelled through the wilderness for four reasons (Numbers 13:27 through 14:34):

1) To develop faith knowing God is able (13:30–31)
2) To be separated to God leaving the world (14:2–4)
3) To learn belief in God's Word (14:6–8)
4) To receive the promises God had made (14:9)

Have you developed these characteristics?

It took forty years because of failures to retain the above attributes (Numbers 14:34). Notice in verse 34 the wording "ye shall know my breach of promise." The word breach in this verse means "alienation or enmity" to actively oppose, not enabling God to fulfill the promise.

It's interesting this same phrase (breach of promise) is used when a man does not fulfill his promise to marry a woman (Jesus our bridegroom—Mark 2:19–20/Matthew 25:1–6).

For let not that man think that he shall receive anything of the Lord. A double minded man is unstable in all his ways.

(James 1:7–8)

Double mindedness causes a person to try and live one life for self and another for God. Vacillating back and forth between the two. Playing the odds between good and evil along the way. Not realizing this is sin and failure toward God.

To not believe God is sin. Overcome evil by believing and accepting the truth of God. Understand that good and evil can be present at the same time, but we don't have to go back and forth between the two.

For I know that in me (that is, in my flesh,) dwelleth no good thing: for the will is present with me; but how to perform that which is good I find not.
For the good that I would I do not: but the evil which I would not, that I do.
Now if I do that I would not, it is no more I that do it, but sin that dwelleth in me.
I find then a law, that, when I would do good, evil is present with me.
For I delight in the law of God after the inward man:
But I see another law in my members, warring against the law of my mind, and bringing me into captivity to the law of sin which is in my members.
O wretched man that I am! Who shall deliver me from the body of this death?
I thank God through Jesus Christ our Lord. So, then with the mind I myself serve the law of God; but with the flesh the law of sin.

(Romans 7:18–25)

Learn to recognize and concur the shuttle differences during internal battles between good and evil. Lean on the word and the fact the Jesus is savior.

As we travel, working through the events of our lives today, we must learn and retain the same four attributes mentioned earlier (faith, be separate, believe the Word of God, and receive the promises of God). We must stay focused on the Lord God, embracing what Jesus Christ has done for us to prevent the benefits and promises of God from being delayed in our life. Notice God's promise was delayed for Israel, not eradicated (to destroy or put an end to).

Don't look back after your deliverance as Lot's wife did during the destruction of Sodom and Gomorrah (Genesis 19:26). Thinking and desiring what has been left behind.

Notice even the children of Israel multiple times when faced with adversity thought of returning (looking back) to Egypt.

Four drivers that cause a look back from where you are:

1) Fear of battle: fight to overcome (Exodus 13:17)
2) The unknown causing to revert to past practices (of the world) believing in what you can see (Exodus 32:1–6)
3) Lack of faith and confidence in God (Numbers 14:3)
4) Faulty leadership influenced by worldly concepts (Deuteronomy 17:14–20)

Enter into God's presence and rest!

In Exodus 33:14 God proclaims He will be present and give rest to Moses and the people of Israel. This is the key to be able not to look back.

Paniym is the Hebrew word used for presence, means "face/countenance." (1)

Peniymah a form of paniym, meaning faceward or within. (2)

Nuwach is the word for rest meaning to be quiet, settled down to gain comfort. (3)

What God is saying in Exodus 33:14 is that His countenance/presence will perform His inward will for Moses and Israel allowing them to be settled and comforted in all situations.

And he said, unto Him, if thy presence go not with me, carry us not up hence.

For wherein shall it be known here that I and thy people have found grace in thy sight? Is it not in that thou goest with us? So, shall we be separated, I and thy people, from all the people that are upon the face of the earth.

And the Lord said unto Moses, I will do this thing also that thou hast spoken: for thou hast found grace in my sight, and I know thee by name.

And he said, I beseech thee shew me thy glory.

(Exodus 33:15–18)

These are powerful verses. God is committing to Moses that the people of Israel (today's Believer) will be separated from all the other people in the earth because of God's presence being with them (His inward will and pleasure). This is meant for you!

As I mentioned in "Insight No. 1," God knows us! He restates it here to Moses saying, "I know thee by name."

Have you asked God to shew you His glory?

Moses wanted to see the glory of God up close and personal but God only let him see His hind parts because no man can see God and live (Exodus 33:19–23). My point is the power of God is with us and within us. I am sure being next to God was a supernatural experience (read Exodus 34:27–39). The world will know we have been with God as we mature in His will and presence.

Come out of the wilderness and the worldly thinking that rules it. Our journey is what develops us into

24

an overcomer. We must have the ability to spiritually reason and not just follow what we are told.

Jesus question to the Pharisees in Matthew 22:41–46 (whose son is Christ's) caused them to think but they did not answer because the answer was against what they wanted and believed.

Why did Jesus weep (read John 11:32–45)? Jesus groaned twice within himself (His Spirit) as he was dealing with Lazarus death. Verse 40 gives us a hint as to why he groaned. It was because of their unbelief.

Do we not accept the Word because it doesn't fit our plain or purpose; do we display unbelief when God is willing to do the impossible?

What are the events in your life when you were not able to spiritually reason (discern) good and evil; right and wrong; impossible and possible? This is what happened when Jesus arrived after Lazarus's death.

Jesus demonstrated the glory and power of God during the event of Lazarus coming from death back to life. This same glory is available to us today.

I have written unto you, fathers, because ye have known him that is from the beginning. I have written unto you, young men, because ye are strong, and the word of God abideth in you, and ye have overcome the wicked one.

Love not the world, neither the things that are in the world. If any man loves the world, the love of the Father is not in him.

For all that is in the world, the lust of the flesh, and the lust of the eyes, and the pride of life, is not of the Father, but is of the world.

And the world passeth away, and the lust thereof: but he that doeth the will of God abideth forever.

(1 John 2:14–17)

This is the purpose of our journey; that purpose is overcoming the world; traveling from death to life (doing the will of God).

Are you stuck in the past, unable to receive what God has already provided?

Are you able to discern the difference between good and evil; with the influences of evil in your daily life. Know this, evil is present to stop you from entering into your destiny.

Know who you are and what belongs to you! If you're not sure consult with the Lord, use the Word to gain spiritual renewal and deliverance. Understand you are on a journey to an abundant life in Christ.

The thief cometh not, but for to steal, and to kill, and to destroy; I am come that they might have life, and that they might have it more abundantly.

(John 10:10)

We must learn from the experiences illustrated in the Bible; the Old Testament is a map for our journey! The reoccurring patterns and types are there to help us along the way. After all, why does history keeps repeating itself? It repeats because humans forget the results of the past; years later we make the same errant decisions of our predecessors.

The number "2" shows there is a difference between good and evil. On day two of creation a firmament was created that divided waters into two parts, the firmament was called heaven. This was the beginning of establishing heaven and earth which lead to the possibility of good and evil, natural and spiritual. The eternal plan of God to return man back to his original position in God, a spiritual being.

What is being confirmed in your life, is it of good or of evil? What choices are you making? And are those choices based on the Word of God? Have you begun your spiritual transformation, opening the door to the promises God has purposed for you? Your journey positions you for greatness!

BORN OF WATER AND THE SPIRIT

The number "3" denotes the trinity; God in three persons. Man created in God's image is also triune.

Verily, verily, I say unto thee, Except a man be born of water and of the Spirit, he cannot enter into the kingdom of God.
That which is born of the flesh is flesh; and that which is born of the Spirit is spirit.
Marvel not that I said unto thee, Ye must be born again.

(John 3:5–7)

And I will pray the Father, and he shall give you another Comforter, that he may abide with you forever;
Even the Spirit of truth; whom the world cannot receive, because it seeth him not, neither knoweth him: but ye know him; for he dwelleth with you, and shall be in you.

(John 14:16–17)

But the Comforter, which is the Holy Ghost, whom the Father will send in my name, he shall teach you all things, and bring all things to your remembrance, whatsoever I have said unto you.

(John 14:26)

Do you have the Holy Ghost?

Ask, and it shall be given you; seek, and ye shall find; knock, and it shall be opened unto you.

(Matthew 7:7)

This verse relates to anything a Believer seeks from God. I encourage you, seek to be filled with the Holy Ghost.

If you are "Born of Water and the Spirit," you will display the fruits of the spirit.

But the fruit of the Spirit is love, joy, peace, longsuffering, gentleness, goodness, faith,
Meekness, temperance; against such there is no law.

(Galatians 5:22–23)

For the fruit of the Spirit is in all goodness and righteousness and truth; Proving what is acceptable unto the Lord.

(Ephesians 5:9–10)

Does the energy and effort you display in your daily life show that you are in union with God by displaying His character? Are you walking in the "Spirit"? If you are you have crucified the flesh with the affections and lusts.

God gives gifts (the Greek word *charisma*) to men through His Spirit. This is favor received from God that causes deliverance with a spiritual endowment providing a miraculous ability within us.

For the gifts and calling of God are without repentance.

(Romans 11:29)

For as we have many members in one body, and all members have not the same office:
So we, being many, are one body in Christ, and every one members one of another.
Having then gifts differing according to the grace that is given to us, whether prophecy, let us prophesy according to the proportion of faith;
Or ministry, let us wait on our ministering: or he that teacheth, on teaching.

(Romans 12:4–7)

Now there are diversities of gifts, but the same Spirit.
And there are differences of administrations, but the same Lord.
And there are diversities of operations, but it is the same God which worketh all in all.
But the manifestation of the Spirit is given to every man to profit withal.
For to one is given by the Spirit the word of wisdom; to another the word of knowledge by the same Spirit;
To another faith by the same Spirit; to another the gifts of healing by the same Spirit;
To another the working of miracles; to another prophecy; to another discerning of spirits; to another divers kinds of tongues; to another the interpretation of tongues:
But all these worketh that one and the selfsame Spirit, dividing to every man severally as he will.

(1 Corinthians 12:4–11)

For us to navigate and be fruitful for the kingdom work of God we need the gifts of the spirit to help us along the way. We need wisdom and discernment to allow us to determine what are the influences and origin of the communications with their intent, coming from the news and the government; as well as from those around us.

As you work out your salvation (your personal journey), today as a Believer in Christ you must remember your origin (you are derived from God) and are now working on the manifestation of the revelation of being re-born as a son or daughter of God.

What are the gifts God has invested in you?

For the earnest expectation of the creature waiteth for the manifestation of the sons of God.

(Romans 8:19)

For the creature itself also shall be delivered from the bondage of corruption into the glorious liberty of the children of God.

(Romans 8:21)

The Greek word for creature in these two verses is ktisis, which is translated the act of creating or the creative act in process. (4)

We are in process of becoming a new creature in Christ (2 Corinthians 5:17), a divine testimony and manifestation.

This insight will link the creation of Adam to what we should be in Christ; a man or woman with superior insights from the "Lord God Almighty," overcoming submissiveness to the influences of sin.

Remember Adam and Eve knew no sin and no shame until they disobeyed God; then they knew they were naked. We have concurred sin consciousness; through Christ, we are victorious. But this does not mean that our willful sinful actions will be covered by the blood of Jesus. We must repent and come back through the grace of God.

God manifested Himself to Israel through their exit from Egypt just as God manifested Himself to us through the crucifixion of Jesus.

When the heavens and earth were finished. On the seventh day God ended the work of His creation and rested (Genesis 2:1–2).

Then the Lord then planted Eden and placed Adam in the garden to dress and keep it. As with Adam; what has God ordained for you to own and develop (dress and keep) in the kingdom of God and naturally? He's developing you now for your eternal future.

And so it will also be in the seven thousandth year of man's existence; the seventh day (Psalms 90:4/2 Peter 3:8—a day is a thousand years), Satan will cease his work (Isaiah 14:10–17, Luke 10:18, Ezekiel 28:13–19) then the new heaven and earth will be brought down from heaven and we will be changed in a moment in a twinkling of an eye we will be like Him (God) (1 Corinthians 15:42–52, Revelation 21:1–7).

Adam was the original image/likeness of God; imitating divine unity and supremacy with God. Yet he was independent and had God's gift of choice. Adam still was the source of God's people in this earth after his exit from the garden.

For since by man came death, by man came also the resurrection of the dead. For as in Adam all die, even so in Christ shall all be made alive.

(1 Corinthians 15:21–22)

And so, it is written, the first man Adam was made a living soul; the last Adam (Jesus) was made a quick-

ening spirit.

Howbeit that was not first which is spiritual, but that which is natural; and afterward that which is spiritual. The first man is of the earth, earthy: the second man is of the Lord from heaven.

(1 Corinthians 15:45–47)

Jesus the second Adam restored us to our rightful place in God spiritually. We now are men and women living in a natural world restored and connected spiritually to God.

God is not purposeless. He has a plan for each of us and foresaw the beginning from the end of the entire creation and for you.

Adam was to rule what God had created and he was created in God's image (Father, Son, Holy Spirit) with the attributes and capabilities of God, while having relationship and communication with God.

I know this because in Genesis 2:19–20, God let Adam name everything in the creation, which speaks to Adam's knowledge and capabilities. In Genesis 3:8–9, the voice of God walked through the garden of Eden and called unto Adam, Where art thou? Showing God's relationship with the man allowing him to be in His presence.

There are consequences for sin. What choices do you make, which causes separation from God? God is seeking you and calling you into relationship?

Right after God gave judgement to the serpent (Genesis 3:14), God spoke the Word for man's deliverance from a fallen state (Genesis 3:15); the first prophecy of Christ restoring what was lost (our authority and relationship with the heavenly Father). Yet judgement was still given to the woman (Genesis 3:16) and to man (Genesis 3:17–19).

Adam's decision to listen to Eve was the first attack on man's position in God. Notice their eyes were not opened until after Adam did eat of the fruit (Genesis 3:6–7). Women have their place in God, yet we must recognize that Satan approached the woman, what was within her that made her the prey of Satan's attack, the answer is in "Insight No. 4."

The man immediately wanted to shift blame (Genesis 3:12) for his failure to lead.

The plan was now set into motion for the grace of God to be demonstrated by the work of Christ on the cross.

Christ delivered us from the penalty of sin and created us a new, back to our origin in God as demonstrated in Adam.

Therefore, if any man be in Christ, he is a new creature: old things are passed away; behold,
All things are become new.
And all things are of God, who hath reconciled
Us to himself by Jesus Christ, and hath given
To us the ministry of reconciliation;
To wit, that God was in Christ, reconciling the
World unto himself, not imputing their trespasses
unto them; and hath committed unto us the word
of reconciliation.

(2 Corinthians 5:17–19)

Just as God placed Adam in Eden with authority and in communion with God. What is His desire for you and your purpose? What capabilities have He instilled in you enabling you to do what no one else can? Most of all He desires for you to know Him and have relationship with Him through Christ Jesus.

God wants to make known His ways unto us as He did for Moses (Psalms 103:7); He gave Moses capability and knowledge through the inspiration of God and the Holy Spirit. This allowed Moses to write the first five books of the Bible, including Genesis the beginning of God's plan for man and earth.

For now, we see through a glass, darkly; but then face to face: now I know in part; but, then shall I know even as also I am known.

(1 Corinthians 13:12)

God knows you and is waiting for you to take hold and move from faith to faith through the gospel of Christ.

For therein (the gospel) is the righteousness of God revealed from faith to faith: as it is written, The just shall live by faith.

(Romans 1:17)

Just as God created something from nothing in the beginning by simply speaking it into existence. Expand the measure of faith that has been given to you through the acceptance of Jesus Christ as savior, which turns our experiences and trials into tools that position us for the destiny that will follow as your relationship is forged with Christ.

"Therefore, being justified by faith, we have peace with God through our Lord Jesus Christ:
By whom also we have access by faith into this Grace wherein we stand, and rejoice in hope of the Glory of God.

And not only so, but we glory in tribulations also:
Knowing that tribulation worketh patience;
And patience, experience; and experience, hope.

(Romans 5:1–4)

Are you in a season learning to understand your position in God? Now that you are born of water (baptism) and of the Spirit (filling of the Holy Ghost), do you know that there's something greater in the kingdom in store for you? Knowing that the initial step in the process is understanding the transition from the first Adam (the natural) to the second Adam (the spiritual) through Jesus Christ. Do you realize the act of baptism symbolizes your resurrection into a new man and a future translation from the dispensation of grace into the dispensation of eternity?

For I know the thoughts that I think towards you, saith the Lord, thoughts of peace, and not of evil, to give you an expected end.
Then shall ye call upon me, and ye shall go and pray unto me, and I will hearken unto you.
And ye shall seek me, and find me, when ye shall search for me with all your heart.
And I will be found of you, saith the Lord; and I will turn away your captivity, and I will gather you from all the nations, and from all the places whither I have driven you, saith the Lord; and I will bring you again into the place whence I caused you to be carried away captive.

(Jeremiah 29:11–14)

Seek the Lord and He will place you back on track toward your expected end. God by His Spirit will help you come out of the bondages the world presents.

In my Father's house are many mansions: if it were not so, I would have told you. I go to prepare a place for you.
And if I go and prepare a place for you, I will come again and receive you unto myself; that where I am, there ye may be also.
And whither I go ye know, and the way ye know.

(John 14:2–4)

Jesus saith, I am the way, the truth and the life: no man cometh unto the Father, but by me.
If ye had known me, ye should have known my Father also; and from henceforth ye know him, and have seen him.

(John 14:6–7)

Who Is God?

"In the beginning God created the heaven and the earth."

(Genesis 1:1)

During the creation process the word God in Hebrew is Elohim. This word is plural (Father, Son, Holy Spirit) in its form. It signifies the supreme and true God. Elohim created the heaven and the earth through the attributes of the Father, the Son (Word) and Holy Spirit.

In Exodus 3:14 after Moses asked God in verse 13, when I say, "The God of your fathers hath sent me; and they ask what is the name, what shall I say to them?"

God said, "I AM THAT I AM; say unto the children of Israel I AM hath sent me." Yahweh is the word for I AM; a variant of the word Jehovah.

God tells Moses in Exodus 6:3 that Abraham, Isaac, and Jacob knew Him as God Almighty "El Shaddai" but they did not know Him as Jehovah (self-existent/eternal).

Who is God? He is Elohim (Father, Son (the Word), and Holy Spirit) the creator of the heavens and earth; He is "Yahweh—I Am"; simply He does exist because He is Jehovah—self-existent and eternal; He is "El Shaddai—the Lord God Almighty." Have you caught a glimpse of who your Father is?

This is the generation of them that seek him (God), that seek thy face, O Jacob. Selah.

(Psalms 24:6)

Check out the entire Twenty-Fourth Psalm:

"And the King of Glory shall come in!"

Let's review a couple of words from John 3:5–7. The word water illustrates a view of being out of water, conveying baptism. Baptism is a symbol not the cause of Believers being identified with Christ. The new birth is demonstrated as we set aside our previous fleshly desires and have an entirely new beginning.

The word spirit means current of air (breath), creating the rational soul in principle and disposition; superhuman capability.

The Spirit is what God breathed into Adam (Genesis 2:7), making him a living soul. Which is also the breath that was breathed within us making us alive again in Christ Jesus, as defined above by the word pneuma.

Through Christ we shall once again be in God's presence.

Even when we were dead in sins, hath quickened us together with Christ, (by grace ye are saved;)
And hath raised us up together, and made us sit together in heavenly places in Christ Jesus:
That in the ages to come he might shew the exceeding riches of his grace in his kindness toward us through Christ Jesus.

(Ephesians 2:5–7)

Quickened in verse 5 means the capability given immediately to respond to spiritual stimuli. There is neither growth or time needed before being able to walk by the spirit. Will give more detail of walking by the Spirit during "Insight No. 5…Listen."

The Spirit is the mighty penetrating power of the invisible God. It is the source of life; the breath of God that kindle the kindred feelings of the divine nature.

Through the Spirit, God is able to communicate life to mankind, who are thus able to feel, think, speak, and act in accordance with the divine will and nature of God.

Blessed be the God and Father or our Lord Jesus Christ, who hath blessed us with all spiritual blessing in heavenly places in Christ.
According as he hath chosen us in him before the foundation of the world, that we should be holy and without blame before him in love:
Having predestinated us unto the adoption of children

*by Jesus Christ to himself, according to the good plea-
sure of his will.*

(Ephesians 1:3–5)

This is a reminder your divine testimony was established before time began. God knew who would
except Him before the world began. But that does not
mean some are destined to salvation and some aren't.
It is each of our choice to make the decision to serve
or not to serve "The Lord God Almighty." He simply
knows who would and who wouldn't.

*The number "3" denotes the trinity; God in three
persons. On day three of creation dry land and earth
appeared with grass, herbs, and fruit. The battle ground
for the man who was created in God's image (triune).*

Are you born of the water and the spirit enabling
you to live out your divine testimony, manifesting the
presence of God in your life?

INSIGHT #4

RESPONSE TO TEMPTATION AND TESTS

The number "4" shows division. The difference in day and night—light and darkness.

From the beginning it's been all about worship. We are challenged through temptation not so God will know our spiritual state but that we will know and recognize our spiritual strengths and weaknesses. Is our spiritual state driven by light or darkness?

A failure to respond as God expects is not the end of our relationship with our Father. It is an opportunity to grow from what happened and overcome a specific tendency that hinders us.

There hath no temptation taken you but such as is common to man: but God is faithful, who will not suffer you to be tempted above that ye are able; but will with the temptation also make a way to escape, that ye may be able to bear it.
Wherefore, my dearly beloved, flee from idolatry.
(1 Corinthians 10:13–14)

Idolatry is all around us today. Within our holiday's and within our individual mind sets that our choice is the most important thing.

Individual choice can be dangerous when it is not

43

governed by us based on the laws of God.

Let's link the me, my, and we syndrome to actions that took place in the Bible, when selfish choice was demonstrated outside the will of God.

The first demonstration was that Lucifer (Satan) desired to ascend into heaven and exalt his throne above the stars of God and thought in his heart that he would be like the "Most High God" (Isaiah 14:12–14). This resulted in him being kicked out of heaven and eventually to be transformed into the man of sin (the anti-Christ of Matthew 24:15).

Please review Revelation 12:1–12 and Isaiah 14:3–16, these verses illustrates the coming end of the devil. This comparison is a good example of what I mentioned about the book of Isaiah being an allegory using Israel to show a picture of the hidden meanings of man's transition back to God. A wonderfully constructed maze/puzzle of the destiny of man and the earth.

In Luke 10:18 Jesus said, "I beheld Satan fall from heaven as lightning." Then He continues to let the disciples know the authority they have in Him.

The second demonstration was in Genesis 11:1–9 when the men of the earth built a city and a tower to reach heaven. This is the same attribute that the devil displayed above. Wanting to make a name for themselves and be equal to God.

The weakness of man due to failures toward God were illustrated in the days of Noah (Genesis 6:5–7) and Elijah (1 Kings 16:31–33). Man's heart was on evil continually and following idolatrous practices in forms of pagan worship. We demonstrate the same attributes through our choices that illustrate we are equal and know better than God?

The House of Representative (Congress) last week (May of 2019) passed a resolution that when persons are sworn in to testify, they no longer will say, "So help me God" as their final statement before they testify. They said, "This was done because there is no place for God or other religious references in governance of the nation."

The removal of concepts related to the law and principles of God is happening all over the country.

Idolatry is worship of images or sins of the mind acted out against the morale laws of God; it is also linked to immorality that causes sins of the flesh. Idolatry brings a person into slavery as they become linked to the ideas that the idol represents.

Wherein in time past ye walked according to the course of this world, according to the prince of the power of the air (Satan), the spirit that now worketh in the children of disobedience:

Among whom also we all had our conversation in times past in the lusts of our flesh, fulfilling the desires of the flesh and of the mind; and were by nature the children of wrath, even as others.

(Ephesians 2:2–3)

This verse reminds us our idolatrous nature is a thing of the past. Though it is being demonstrated by others now and was demonstrated by others before us.

Idolatry happens when we conform to the world, its thoughts and practices. It is caused when there is a lack of knowledge or gratitude toward God as we submit ourselves and actions to anything other than the Lord God.

45

My people are destroyed for lack of knowledge: because thou hast rejected knowledge, I will also reject thee, that thou shalt be no priest to me: seeing thou hast forgotten the law of thy God, I will also forget thy children.

(Hosea 4:6)

A downfall for man today is that we don't realize God's judgement is not always immediate. As in the verse above the result of the parent's actions impacted the lives of the children. This is why it's difficult for the natural man to associate the results of sin to events that occur because of God's judgement.

Look at Israel in the book of Jeremiah. Chasing after idolatry and immorality; not heeding to Jeremiah's warnings.

Review 2 Kings chapter 24, 2 Chronicles chapter 36, and Jeremiah chapter 21 to see how the warnings of the king of the north (Nebuchadnezzar) was given years in advance.

In Jeremiah 25:9, God called Nebuchadnezzar His servant. A man being used to fulfill the will of God in Judgement on Israel.

I will now compare and distinguish the types of tests Adam, Eve, and Job experienced in relation to the temptation of Jesus in Matthew 4:1–11.

These tests are the basic stimulus that place individual in a state of idolatry. A state of worship influenced and driven by something other than the laws and the morale character of God.

Please read these verses in Matthew (4:1–11) before you precede and refer back to the verses mentioned in each of the four temptations of Christ.

Matthew 4:1–4: Physical Needs and Wants

The attack of Satan on Job was centered around Job's possessions, family, and health, physical needs. We see the sudden attack on all that Job had. Notice how this happened (Job 1:11–21). Some of it happened by the hands of man, some was by supernatural events (fire from heaven) and some was by environmental occurrences.

In verses 11 and 12 the Lord tells Satan he can touch all that he has but not Job. His oxen, sheep, asses, camels, are taken or killed; then his sons and daughters were killed.

Everything taken from Job were resources to support his physical needs, wants and family. But Job's response was perfect; he showed his grief, but yet gave God reverence.

Then Job arose, and rent has mantle, and shaved his head, and fell down upon the ground, and worshipped, And said, naked came I out of my mother's womb, and naked shall I return thither: The Lord gave, and the Lord hath taken away; blessed be the name of the Lord.
(Job 1:20–21)

Job's successful response caused Satan to ask God to go a step further, to attack his health in chapter 2.

We will discuss Job in Insight No. 8 of this work; you will see it wasn't all about Job's life decisions as much as it was about showing the interaction between God, man and Satan to accomplish the Lord's will in the earth and in our lives.

The key is not to let needs and wants take you into errant decisions to fulfilling those desires. How is this controlled? Depend on God for the answer; cast all your cares on Him for He cares for you.

Matthew 4:5–7: God's Word Manipulated

Eve wanted a greater position, her ambition and self-centered ways lead her to question what God had said, "Don't eat lest ye die." The serpent inserted the thought of doubt of God's Word by saying, "Ye shall not surely die."

They did not die naturally but they died spiritually and lost communion and the presence of God (Genesis 3:22–24).

We should not tempt God by doubting or testing His word for selfish authentication. If Christ had cast himself off the pinnacle, He would have been led by the will of the devil to prove God and possibly may have died in the process. Eliminating the avenue of salvation through His crucifixion.

Matthew 4:8–10: Prestige, Control, and Idolatry

I asked the question in "Insight No. 3"; what was in the woman that made her the prey of Satan? Eve wanted to elevate her standing in the creation model. Our adversary (Satan) also wanted to be elevate above his place in the creation (Isaiah 14:14).

The serpent enticed Eve by telling her she would not die but become like gods knowing good and evil (Genesis 3:3–5). The fruit was good food; pleasant to eyes, able to make one wise (Genesis 3:6).

See how Satan used the visual of the tree and fruit to entice Eve; just as he enticed Jesus with the visual of all the kingdoms of the world. The devil desired to create a lust in Eve and Jesus to be greater. Let God take you to your greater end, follow Christ Jesus, the name above every name, resulting in every knee bowing (in earth and under the earth) and every tongue confessing that He is Lord (Philippians 2:10–11).

Eve's action was an act of idolatry by wanting to be as a god; therefore, she submitted herself to the rule of another bringing herself into slavery becoming linked to the ideas that the idol represents.

We don't know everything about Eve's role in relation to Adam's headship, but we do know she was to be his help meet (Genesis 2:20). Help meet is to aid or help.

Adam followed Eve into disobedience; becoming a willing participant.

Man was pure with thoughts of good. He knew no shame because of lust, selfishness, or rebellion against God.

This is how they became like God: by knowing disobedience to God was possible and understanding the shame of sin that brings about eternal separation from God, which the devil had already experienced. It also brings about the reality of living in a lower state spiritually; not as the man God created, but as a man with a mindset of inferior thinking.

Adam and Eve lost eternity and the tree of life, the Word which is Jesus Christ. The Living Word keeping the way of the tree of life.

So, he drove out the man; and he placed at the East of the garden of Eden Cherubims, and a flaming sword which turned every way, to keep the way of the tree of life.

(Genesis 3:24)

For the word of God is quick, and powerful, and sharper than any twoedged sword, piercing even to the dividing asunder of soul and spirit, and of the joints and marrow, and is a discerner of the thoughts and intents of the heart.

(Hebrews 4:12)

Only the Word can separate and identify the thoughts that come from the inner-man.

Can you see the similarity of the above two scriptures (the sword is the Word)? Adam's failure caused the loss of the working of the Word of God within his soul resulting in spiritual separation from God. Remember earlier in this work I mentioned the voice of God walked in the garden (Genesis 3:8–9).

The Word of God must be preserved, because it is how we overcome our advisory the devil causing him to flee and understand our position in God. This was demonstrated in Matthew 4:1–11.

The pope said, "He would change the words in the example Jesus gave us on how to pray from lead us not into temptation" (Matthew 6:13), because it gives the inference that God leads us into temptation. Temptation in this verse is the Greek word "peirasmos" meaning trials divinely permitted with a beneficial purpose (5) permitted by God, but God is not the source of the trial. Just as God permitted Satan to test Job.

The trials in this verse speaks of sources outside or beyond our control. If the pope changes this verse, he basically will be removing the concept that we will be tried in our walk with God. We must be overcomers in those moments of trial to demonstrate our growth in God's Word (Christ).

Christ made it possible for us to once again partake of the tree of life. The indwelling of the Word creating us a new into the image of God.

Temptation shows areas in our life we must concur. Just as Job's fears came upon him, the test the Lord allowed enabled him to learn from that experience.

The Lord is helping us through our experiences to overcome fears and weaknesses.

Wherefore as the Holy Ghost saith, today if ye will hear his voice,
Harden not your hearts, as in the provocation, in the day of temptation in the wilderness.

(Hebrews 3:7–8)

My brethren, count it all joy when ye fall into divers' temptations;
Knowing this, that the trying of your faith worketh patience.
But let patience have her perfect work, that ye may be perfect and entire, wanting nothing.

(James 1:2–4)

Are you struggling with temptation? Are you saying what God's Word says about the situation?

Know who you are in God, consult with the Lord concerning every issue in your life, and use the Word of God to overcome temptations just as Christ did in Matthew 4:1–10.

Study to shew thyself approved unto God, a workman that needeth not to be ashamed, rightly dividing the word of truth.

(2 Timothy 2:15)

51

Matthew 4:11: Angels Ministered

Just as Satan told Christ, "Didn't God give His angels charge over you?" Recognize the ministry of the Holy Ghost toward you and realize the angels are able to protect you from evil, natural and spiritual.

Are they not all ministering spirits, sent forth to minister for them who shall be heirs of salvation?
(Hebrews 1:14)

Practice the example of Christ in Matthew 4:1–11. Use the Word of God in times of temptation and testing. Use the Word of God to define your reality.

The number "4" shows division. The difference in day and night; light and darkness. On day four of creation God created the sun, moon, and stars; giving each rule over their space in time. Did you know most all idolatry stated with the worship of the sun, moon, and stars?

Overcome internal struggles by quoting and focusing on the Word of God related to the temptation or test. Then the devil will depart from trying to cause your separation from God. Light drives out darkness. Our light is the Word of God, it's a light unto our path (Psalms 119:105).

LISTEN

The number "5" is symbolic of grace.

Hear His Voice!

To understand God and His grace we must learn to hear Him speaking to us and be directed by the guidance of the Holy Spirit.

First Kings 19:11–13: when the Lord passed by there was wind, earthquake and fire due to his presence but the Lord was not in any of these signs. After all of this, when the fire ended there was a *still small voice* that spoke to Elijah asking him why he was there in the cave.

Are you in a cave, isolated by fear and doubt? Have the issues of life or the events happening in our nation hindering you from hearing God?

Learn to overcome all the noise that life puts in front of you, lies by the media, manipulation by the government, racial and social strife (wind, earthquake and fire) and focus on what God says in His Word and the direction He confirms for you to take through the Holy Spirit. Learn to listen and recognize His voice speaking to you through the Holy Ghost, because He is a gentleman, He will not over shadow everything that's going on in your mind and life (He speaks in a still small voice).

Seek God's presence in your life, Moses and Elijah had personal one on one conversations with the God of the universe and you can also!

Heirs!

The Spirit bears witness with our spirit, that we are the children of God. This means we are heirs of God and joint-heirs with Christ. (Romans 8:16–17). Being willing to be different (God like) and suffer the rejection of the world.

Heirs have rights!

Line up your thoughts with His Word and pray for God to direct you!

God's thoughts toward you have an expectation of achievement. He is wanting you to call to him, then He will hear you and answer your cry. You will find Him as you seek for Him with all your heart.

Then you will know and recognize His voice when He speaks!

That which was from the beginning, which we have heard, which we have seen with our eyes, which we have looked upon, and our hands have handled, of the Word of life;

(For the life was manifested, and we have seen it, and bear witness, and shew unto you that eternal life, which was with the Father, and was manifested unto us;)

That which we have seen and heard declare we unto you, that ye also may have fellowship with us; and truly our fellowship is with the Father, and with his Son Jesus Christ.

And these things write we unto you, that your joy may be full.

(1 John 1:1–4)

Along the journey listen to the Spirit of God. *We must know* what God is speaking to the Believer of today through the Spirit. That the manifestation of His grace and redemption is performed through our daily lives. Don't let the situations of life blind you and prevent you from hearing God through the Holy Ghost.

The word heard in 1 John 1:1; means more than hearing words or sounds, it indicates understanding the meaning of what is said.

Now the Spirit speaketh expressly, that in the latter times some shall depart from the faith, giving heed to seducing spirits, and doctrines of devils;

Speaking lies in hypocrisy; having their conscience seared with a hot iron.

(1 Timothy 4:1–2)

We are in a period of time in the history of man where we have a form of Godliness but deny the power of God (2 Timothy 3:1–6).

People say we believe in God, but their view is of a God that is tolerant to the ungodly acts and beliefs of men. That God gave us a choice, therefore who and what we are is up to us; with the belief that in the end He will accept us. After all Christ died for our sins.

This is errant thinking and a denial of the power of God to change us by the washing of the Word, making us anew each day becoming more like Him.

So, then faith cometh by hearing and hearing by the Word of God.

(Romans 10:17)

Hearing is the Greek word akoe, the act or sense of hearing. (6)

When you pray do you hear the Lord's response?

I hear His responses mainly through scripture (the Word). You must believe He is acting on what's asked; faith is more than hearing the Word being quoted and then requoting it. It is hearing God's response with in your spirit and knowing He is acting on that response because we believe.

In the beginning was the Word, and the Word was with God, and the Word was God.
The same was in the beginning with God. All things were made by Him; and without Him was not anything made that was made.
In Him was life; and the life was the light of men.
(John 1:1–4)

The revelation of Christ is understanding that He is the active power of the Godhead and His death allowed that ability to be transferred to the Believer. We are baptized into Him, which is the Word; the creative power of God.

Logos is the Greek word used here for Word in John 1:1. Logos denotes the expression of thought (the thoughts of God).(7)

The heavens and earth were created after the thoughts of God were spoken. He thought it (*logos*) and then said it (*rhema*).

Jesus made all things, bringing life during creation and now eternal life through salvation (John 1:3–4).

But as many as received Him, to them gave them power to become the sons of God, even to them that believe on His Name.
(John 1:12)

We are bound to give thanks always to God for you, brethren beloved of the Lord, because God hath from the beginning chosen you to salvation through sanctification of the Spirit and belief of the truth.

(2 Thessalonians 2:13)

Belief and the act of believing are derived from faith. Faith means to have trust in divine things, conviction of truth with relationship to God. Therefore, faith can't be activated without belief or personal conviction that a thing is true.

But what saith it? The word is nigh thee, even in thy mouth, and in thy heart: that is the word of faith, which we preach;
That if thou shalt confess with thy mouth the Lord Jesus, and shalt believe in thine heart that God hath raised him from the dead, thou shalt be saved.
For with the heart man believeth unto righteousness; and with the mouth confession is made unto salvation.
(Romans 10:8–10)

The Spirit gives witness to the ability of Christ to provide salvation. We must realize our sanctification and salvation were authored through the word of truth. And that truth is Jesus Christ; the Living Word.

Your confession of Christ creates the elements of grace, redemption and salvation in our life.

So is being a son/daughter of God about salvation? Yes, but there is much more. Being a son or daughter means you have the benefits of your father. Do you understand your benefit plan?

And it shall come to pass, that before they call, I will answer; and while they are speaking, I will hear.

(Isaiah 65:24)

This prophecy can be activated now; it is part of the benefits of being a son or daughter of the King.

For in Him dwelleth all the fulness of the Godhead bodily. And ye are complete in Him, which is the head of all principality and power:

(Colossians 2:9–10)

Who being the brightness of His glory, and the express image of His person, upholding all things by the Word of His power, when He had himself purged our sins, sat down on the right hand of the Majesty on high.

(Hebrews 1:3)

I like the way Luke describes how Jesus received the fulness of the Godhead:

Now when all the people were baptized, it came to pass, that Jesus also being baptized, and praying, the heavens was opened, and the Holy Ghost descended in a bodily shape like a dove upon Him, and a voice came from heaven, which said, Thou art my beloved Son; in thee I am well pleased.

(Luke 3:21–22)

The Holy Ghost descended on Jesus in the shape of a body completing the fulness of the Godhead bodily in human form.

Have you ever thought the fulness of the Godhead operated in you (Father, Son, Holy Ghost)?

Are you "*listening*" and hearing with understanding?

But we all, with open face beholding as in a glass the glory of the Lord, are changed into the same image from glory to glory, even as by the Spirit of the Lord.
(2 Corinthians 3:18)

Glory is the self-manifestation of what God does; it is exhibited in how He reveals Himself. What has God revealed to you from the time when you first believed; are you moving from glory to glory? Seeing yourself being changed into the image of Christ with the fulness of His capability. Are you preparing yourself to be ready for what the Lord God is about to do through His people?

You are born of God; not of blood, nor of the will of the flesh, nor of the will of man, but of God (1 John 1:13).

Born to move from glory to glory, through experience by experience, providing documentation after documentation creating a recorded of the acts of God on your behalf at each level of your growth.

And hath raised us up together, and made us sit in heavenly places in Christ Jesus; That in the ages to come He might shew the exceeding riches of His grace in His kindness toward us through Christ Jesus.
(Ephesians 2:6–7)

Now unto him that is able to do exceedingly and abundantly above anything we can ask or think because of the power within us.
(Ephesians 3:20)

The word *power* in this verse is the Greek word "*dunamis*" meaning miraculous power (8), which resides in a person waiting to be released as God gives the inspiration.

We are new creatures predestined to be conformed to His image.

(Romans 8:29)

The development of our faith is the avenue for our growth and development in God. As we act on and confess what we hear from the Word of God, it produces the results in our lives that demonstrate the creating of something from nothing as we believe what we speak. This can't be done without the unction of the Holy Ghost, causing you to know all things (1 John 2:20) doing all things that are in the executable will of God (Matthew 21:19–22).

Don't think or focus on what you see.

Now faith is the substance of things hoped for, and the evidence of things not seen.

(Hebrews 11:1)

We are bound to give thanks always to God for you, brethren beloved of the Lord, because God hath from the beginning chosen you to salvation through sanctification of the Spirit and belief of the truth.

(2 Thessalonians 2:13)

Belief and the act of believing are derived from faith. Faith means to have trust in divine things, conviction of truth with relationship to God. Therefore, faith can't be activated without belief or personal conviction that a thing is true.

We must realize our sanctification and salvation were offered through the word of truth. And that truth is Jesus Christ.

If we confess what God says in the Word, it builds our faith once we hear it. Hearing is when by unction of the Holy Ghost, faith and belief are developed within you.

Let the facts of who you are always be nigh thee, and even in your mouth; that through confession it becomes reality. The reality of being redeemed by the grace of God, which results in miraculous power (dunamis) on our behalf.

I was reminded of the following statement; the Lord orders the path of those who don't lean to their own understanding (Proverbs 3:5–6).

The baptism that Jesus was baptized with (the express image of God's person with a record of execution of His will in heaven) has not been seen in our generation but it is about to happen causing the release of God's capability and His power! Amen and Amen! (So be it.)

Have your listening skills been sharpened? Are you able to recognize and understand what the Holy Ghost is speaking to you?

Improve your communication skill with God by learning to listen with understanding what the Spirit of God is saying. We hear through the unction (chrisma) of the Holy Ghost:

But ye have an unction from the Holy One, and ye know all things.

(1 John 2:20)

But the anointing which ye have received of him abideth in you, and ye need not that any man teach you: but as the same anointing teacheth you of all things, and is truth, and is no lie, and even as it hath taught you, ye shall abide in him.

(1 John 2:27)

The unction of the Holy Ghost is the smearing, the endowment of the anointing; the anointing is what bears witness to truth within your spirit and lets you know this is God speaking.

Chrisma (unction) and *Charisma* (gifts) both fall under the operation (function) of the Holy Spirit to be used to lead and guide us through use of gifts or confirming truth through His presence.

If your communication abilities are not what they should be then: ask, and it shall be given you; seek, and ye shall find; knock, and it shall be opened unto you.

For the word of God is quick, and powerful, and sharper than any twoedged sword, piercing even to the dividing asunder of the soul and spirit, and of the joints and marrow, and is a discerner of the thoughts and intents of the heart.

(Hebrews 4:12)

The Word and the Spirit of God works together to deal with the inner man. There is nothing not manifested in His sight and all things are naked and open unto Him.

Without His grace we are failures. *Listen* to the directions of God by His Spirit—fast and pray and you will discover the redemptive power of God; through seeking God, asking that the doors of your mind become open and sensitive to the internal voice of the Spirit of God within you.

Know this whatsoever you ask of God in Jesus Name, it shall be done (John 14:13). The Spirit of truth will dwell within you enabling your ability to hear what the Spirit of God is saying unto the Church. Amen!

The number "5" is symbolic of grace. On day five of creation God created the creatures of the sea and of the air. Displaying His benevolence and grace toward earth through the creation of the first living creatures.

INSIGHT #6

HEAVEN AND EARTH

The number "6" denotes man without God.
I made this comment in Insight No. 5, "born to move from glory to glory, through experience by experience, providing documentation after documentation creating *a recorded* of the acts of God on your behalf at each level of your growth."

This is the essence of this chapter. The records and documentation of heaven being testified, witnessed and demonstrated in the earth, overcoming imperfection and evil.

That the God of our Lord Jesus Christ, the Father of glory, may give unto you the spirit of wisdom and revelation in the knowledge of him:
The eyes of your understanding being enlightened; that ye may know what is the hope of his calling, and what the riches of the glory of his inheritance in the saints,
And what is the exceeding greatness of his power to us-ward who believe, according to the working of his mighty power,
Which he wrought in Christ, when he raised him from the dead, and set him at his own right hand in the heavenly places,
Far above all principality, and power, and might, and

dominion, and every name that is named, not only in this world, but also in that which is to come.

(Ephesians 1:17–21)

Because of the reality of the above scripture; this scripture is our destination:

Therefore, leaving the principles of the doctrine of Christ, let us go on unto perfection; not laying again the foundation of repentance from dead works, and of faith toward God.

(Hebrews 6:1)

Even though man is imperfect in our current state, we must remember before the world was formed, we were destined to be God's spiritual representatives; the mind and heart of God thought of us and created us in His image (a spiritual being). Now in this natural state we have the ability to go on to perfection. Moving past the principle doctrines of Christ as the heaven and earth is being transitioned to the New Jerusalem with a new heaven and a new earth (Revelation 21:1–3).

Overcome the present evil, anything exalting itself above instruction from God in our paths, moving into perfection through and in Christ.

For there are three that bear record in heaven, the Father, the Word, and the Holy Ghost: and these three are one.
And there are three that bear witness in earth, the spirit, and the water, and the blood: and these three agree in one.

(1 John 5:7–8)

66

In the prior insight, we discussed Jesus as the Word; the living Word of God and He is the Word in verse 7 above bearing record within the God Head of what God has spoken in the future.

This insight discusses the Holy Ghost documenting the record in heaven and the Spirit bearing witness in the earth of the documented plan and acts of God through us. Notice there are two independent functions of the Spirit of God. The Holy Ghost bearing record in heaven of the established truth and the Spirit bearing witness of the record from heaven in the earth.

In verse 7 the *Holy Ghost* is referenced in heaven and bears record: a record affirms what has been experienced and documented; like a court reporter in a trial.

The Holy Ghost in Heaven supports the validity of the record recorded in Heaven of God's initial purpose of man and His creation. This is the distinction of what we will witness during the coming demonstration of what the Lord God will perform through the Believer. Having the full power of the Godhead behind and within us.

We must remember this record is a link to the opening of the books in heaven.

And I saw the dead, small and great, stand before God; and the books were opened: and another book was opened, which is the book of life: and the dead were judged out of those things which were written in the books, according to their works.

(Revelation 20:12)

This is all of our works, the works performed by the administration of the Holy Ghost within us and the works we perform from our selfish and fleshly desires.

This is not a judgement to determine if the Believer will go to heaven or hell. It is part of the process to determine what foundation have you built on. Did you realize there is a record established and your works would be tried?

Every man's work shall be made manifest: for the day shall declare it, because it shall be revealed by fire, and the fire shall try every man's work of what sort it is.
(1 Corinthians 3:13)

How do you respond to challenges? Will your responses and actions survive the test of fire? Will your activity in God's kingdom prove to be a reflection of the purposes of God's plan for you?

That the trial of your faith, being much more precious than of gold that perisheth, though it be tried with fire, might be found unto praises and honour and glory at the appearing of Jesus Christ.
(1 Peter 1:7)

We must begin to see ourselves through the lens of the Lord through what the Holy Ghost has affirmed for us from heaven. Not on what is seen or understood in the realm of the earth. Know that your capability in God is abundant more than you have ever imaged. Begin to realize your progression from faith to faith and glory to glory.

Faith in God's plan begins with hope and is derived from the invisible.

Now faith is the substance of things hoped for, the evidence of things not seen.
(Hebrews 11:1)

The word *substance* is the visual connection with in our minds that creates the mental picture for our benefit to illustrate what we are asking (just as God did when He created the earth).

Hupostasis the Greek word for substance signifies a setting or standing under, a foundation (9), meaning the thing hoped for is supported by the Father, the Word (Jesus) and the Holy Ghost; *please grasp and understand this fact.*

The substance of what's hoped for is revealed and brought to reality as we stand under the testimony of the record established by God, our foundation. Based on the practice and power of faith established before the beginning of time.

Do you believe it is possible from the start of time for God to know everything you would need and ask thousands of years in the future?

But when you pray, use not vain repetitions, as the heathen do; for they think that they shall be heard for their much speaking.

Be not ye therefore like unto them; for your Father knoweth what things ye have need of, before ye ask Him.

(Matthew 6:7–8)

So the possibility of answer to prayers being known by God before we ask is a fact. The answer is established in heaven before you ask. Even at times we hope for a different answer.

The Greek word for evidence in Hebrews 11:1 is elegchos meaning proof and conviction (10), which provides the evidence. That means evidence is developed from the conviction that God is true and He can and will perform what we ask, yet the evidence is not seen but has been established, already formed in the heavens, based on what we have heard and seen God perform in the past (the record is written in heaven). This is our proof. But it takes the Spirit of God to confirm it within us through the unction of the Spirit.

The Father, the Word, and the Holy Ghost created the heavens and earth from nothing, this is evidence and the record of who we are; and the ability of God working through us was established from the beginning, not when the earth was formed but, in the beginning, when it was first thought of by God, before Lucifer said, "He would exalt his throne above the stars of God and be like most High" (Isaiah 14:12–15).

This is why even though "6" denotes manifestation of evil, man without God and the man of sin 666 (Revelation 13:18), falling short of God's perfectness; we can be perfect because of the record established in heaven for us.

The Spirit in 1 John 5:8 is referenced in the earth and bears witness of truth through salvation (Christ baptism and crucifixion), a witness testifies of the evidence that an event occurred making it a reality.

He that believeth on the Son of God hath the witness in himself: he that believeth not God hath made him a liar; because he believeth not the record that God gave of his Son.
And this is the record, that God hath given to us eternal life, and this life is in his Son.
(1 John 5:10–11)

The Spirit confirms the truth of Christ in the earth, but the Holy Ghost states facts and details of the record documented in heaven. The Holy Ghost teaches us through the Spirit the knowledge of God by divine revelation and inspiration. The knowledge of God is not knowing about Him; it is the knowledge that God has.

But the Comforter, which is the Holy Ghost, whom the Father will send in my name, He shall teach you all things, and bring all things to your remembrance, whatsoever I have said unto you.

(John 14:26)

But when the Comforter is come, whom I will send unto you from the Father, even the Spirit of truth, which proceedeth from the Father, He shall testify of me:
(John 15:26)

This is the transition we will experience as the Lord God inspires the Believers of today. The testimony of Christ and understanding truth from heaven as the Spirit confirms teachings straight from the mouth and heart of God. Transitioning from knowledge of Jesus as savior; to knowledge of Him as the living Word in demonstration through the knowledge of God (through the knowledge that God has) as we end the sixth day of the creations and enter the seventh.

The Witness (1 John 5:8)

And there are three that bear witness in earth, the spirit, and the water, and the blood: and these three agree in one.

(1 John 5:8)

Let's look at the three verses prior to 1 John 5:7–8.

71

For whatsoever is born of God overcometh the world; and this is the victory that overcometh the world, even our faith.

Who is he that overcometh the world, but he that believeth that Jesus is the Son of God?

This is he that came by water and blood, even Jesus Christ; not by water only, but by water and blood. And it is the Spirit that beareth witness, because the Spirit is truth.

(1 John 5:4–6)

The sacrifice of Christ was the greatest witness to man of God's love. It set into motion our future in God.

Our faith in Jesus Christ gives us victory in every situation, that we can encounter in this world.

Put off the former conversation of the old man, and be renewed in the spirit of your mind, that ye will put on the new man, which is after God created in righteousness and true holiness.

(Ephesians 4:21–24)

And be not conformed to this world: but be ye transformed by the renewing of your mind, that ye may prove what is that good, and acceptable, and perfect, will of God.

(Romans 12:2)

Work to overcome the limitations of our human make up and allow the fulness of the Lord God to be functioning in your life. Let each experience build your confidence and develop your faith.

Heaven's Record Brought to Earth

We will need the fulness of God as we enter into the coming season of the existence of the world, with all its deception and unrighteousness.

Fast and Pray!

Our prayers must display confidence in God's ability to perform.

After this manner therefore pray ye: Our Father which art in heaven, Hallowed be thy name.
Thy kingdom come, Thy will be done in earth, as it is in heaven.

(Matthew 6:9–10)

Jesus starts by tell us to recognize God as the Holy and Sanctified one (Hallowed be thy name). We should give praise and thanks to God as we make our request known to Him (Philippians 4:6).

He then tells us in prayer to recognize the Father for bringing His kingdom and His will from heaven to earth. The record established in heaven to be revealed in the earth.

In verse 13 of Matthew chapter 6, Jesus's demonstrated prayer ends by asking not to be led into temptation and being delivered from evil.

This concept in prayer, victory over temptation and evil to obtain abundant life goes all the way back to Jabez.

And Jabez called on the God of Israel, saying, Oh that thou wouldest bless me indeed, and enlarge my coast, and that thine hand might be with me, and that thou

*wouldest keep me from evil, that it may not grieve me!
And God granted him that which he requested.*

(1 Chronicles 4:10)

We must begin to understand the evil spiritual influence of the world can hinder our functional capabilities in God. But first we must realize that there are evil spiritual influencing driving the thoughts and intents of this world. We can't ignore its presence, if we do, we open ourselves to seducing lying spirits that promote tolerance of things that are ungodly.

When we think of evil, we envision things on the extreme like mass murder. But evil once again can be anything that opposes the will of God.

Things that oppose God's will, no matter how small can hinder our capability to recognize good and evil.

In John 17:13–24 Jesus prayed for us to the father that He not take us out of the world, but sanctify us through the Word of truth, and that we become one even as they are (the God Head). Then He states a fact that we haven't seen in our generation: Jesus said, that the glory God gave Him, "be given to us," being made perfect in oneness.

Oneness with the Father and the Son (Jesus) requires us (Believers) to also become one. This is the key to overcoming the manifestation of evil and becoming perfect. Jesus asked that the glory God demonstrated through Him and the future glory of eternity be given to us. *Please read John 17:13–24.*

Listen, we are seeing the world fall head long into the deceptiveness of the practices of Satan more every day.

During this time of transition from imperfection

to perfection, the following scripture is ever more important.

Yea, if thou criest after knowledge, and liftest up thy voice for understanding;
If thou seekest her as silver, and searchest for her as for hid treasures;
Then shalt thou understand the fear of the Lord, and find the knowledge of God.
For the Lord giveth wisdom: out of his mouth cometh knowledge and understanding.
He layeth up sound wisdom for the righteous: he is a buckler to them that walk uprightly.
He keepeth the paths of judgment, and preserveth the way of his saints.
Then shalt thou understand righteousness, and judgment, and equity; yea, every good path.
(Proverbs 2:3–9)

The number "6" denotes man without God. On day six of creation God created living creatures such as bugs, cattle, and all the other beasts of the earth. Then he made man also to populate the earth. During "Insight #1" I mentioned the concept that the men and women created on day six, was not Adam, which possessed a living soul.

We can be perfect in God overcoming evil, possessing our newfound life as we are transformed from the natural to the spiritual, becoming one with God manifesting His attributes.

INSIGHT #7

KEYS TO THE KINGDOM

The number "7" represents perfection.
The first six insights of this work were to bring you to this point of how to operate in the kingdom of God. A time to represent and manifest the creator in your life.

And I will give unto thee the keys of the kingdom of heaven: and whatsoever thou shalt bind on earth shall be bound in heaven: and whatsoever thou shalt loose on earth shall be loosed in heaven.
(Matthew 16:19)

The prior insight "Heaven and Earth" was a segue into why Matthew 16:19 works. The record in heaven as witnessed in earth.

Verses 17 and 18 mentions Simon Barjona's name was to be Peter (*petros*, meaning a rock or stone) because God revealed to him that Jesus was Christ, the son of God. The word rock in verse 18 is *petra* meaning a massive rock that the church would be built on, this massive rock is Jesus who Peter recognized as Christ.

The word *keys* are the Greek word *kleis*, a key with ability to open up the kingdom to man through the door of faith. (11)

The word *kingdom* is the Greek word *basileia* representing the realm of sovereignty and royal power of God within His kingdom. (12) The word *bind/bound* is *deo* meaning to bind or tie in bonds. (13) *Loose/loosen* is *luo* meaning to loosen, unloose, unbind, or release. (14)

You have been given by Christ the rock on which the church is built the ability to open the door through faith to the sovereign power of God's kingdom. With the ability to bind/put in bonds things against the will of God and loosen or release the things that are in the will of God.

This is spiritual warfare with the force of God being exercised!

And from the days of John the Baptist until now the kingdom of heaven suffereth violence, and the violent take it by force.

(Matthew 11:12)

This verse illustrates that we must seize the kingdom; forcing our way into what is ours. Then we can experience the force/power of God as illustrated in Phillips translation from Gaza to Azotus (Acts 8:39) and the Apostle Paul's visit to the third heaven (2 Corinthians 12:2).

A struggle for control of the earth and the people that dwell here is happening right before our eyes.

Many of us don't realize that many of the powerful and non-powerful people in this earth actions are being influenced in the spiritual realm. Insight No. 8 will give an example of this. Please consider reading 2 Thessalonians chapter 2 in its entirety.

Let no man deceive you by any means (of the day of Christs return): for that day shall not come, except there come a falling away first, and that man of sin be revealed, the son of perdition;

Who opposeth and exalteth himself above all that is called God, or that is worshipped; so that he as God sitteth in the temple of God, shewing himself that he is God.

Remember ye not, that, when I was yet with you, I told you these things?

And now ye know what withholdeth that he might be revealed in his time.

For the mystery of iniquity doth already work: only he who now letteth will let, until he be taken out of the way.

And then shall the Wicked be revealed, whom the Lord shall consume with the spirit of his mouth, and shall destroy with the brightness of his coming.

(2 Thessalonians 2:3–8)

Verse 7 is speaking of the grace of God working by the Holy Ghost on the hearts of man that is withholding the anti-christ incarnation on earth as a man until the grace of God is no longer operative because of the Holy Ghost is removed from the earth.

Our natural thought process is the enemy because it is not subject to the law of God (Romans 8:7).

For the weapons of our warfare are not carnal, but mighty through God to the pulling down of strong holds;

Casting down imaginations, and every high thing that exalteth itself against the knowledge of God, and bringing into captivity every thought to the obedience of Christ.

(2 Corinthians 10:4–5)

This is why the carnal mind is God's enemy. It prevents man from pulling down strong holds through binding and loosing and bringing our imaginations and thoughts under subjection to Christ (the Living Word of God).

There are religious and spiritual thought processes influencing our walk that men support, which takes away the key of knowledge that enables the Believer to enter this realm of reflecting our creator through Christ because they have not entered into it, therefore it must not be a reality (Luke 11:52).

I Pray That You...

Be strong in the Lord, and the power of his might.
Put on the whole armour of God, that ye may be able to stand against the wiles of the devil.
For we wrestle not against flesh and blood, but against principalities, against powers, against the rulers of the darkness of this world, against spiritual wickedness in high places.
Wherefore take unto you the whole armour of God, that ye may be able to withstand in the evil day, and having done all, to stand.
Stand therefore, having your loins girt about with truth, and having on the breastplate of righteousness;
And your feet shod with the preparation of the gospel of peace;
Above all, taking the shield of faith, wherewith ye shall be able to quench all the fiery darts of the wicked.
And take the helmet of salvation, and the sword of the

Spirit, which is the Word of God:
Praying always with all prayer and supplication in the
Spirit, and watching thereunto with all perseverance
and supplication for all saints.

(Ephesians 6:10–18)

We are covered by God and ready for battle. Learn to use the weapons of our warfare, believe in the Lord God Almighty and His Christ, believe and bind yourself in His truth, know you are made the righteousness of God through Christ, let your steps be guided with the gospel; letting the peace of God rule in your heart, take hold of faith; even the size of a grain of mustard seed will work, guard your mind knowing Christ has delivered you, and use the Word of God as a weapon as Jesus did (remember Insight No. 4).

Jesus said the works I do you shall do also and greater works because I go to the Father (John 14:12–15).

Speak the Word and have faith in God.

For verily I say unto you, That whosoever shall say
unto this mountain, Be thou removed, and be thou cast
into the sea; and shall not doubt in his heart, but shall
believe that those things which he saith shall come to
pass; he shall have whatsoever he saith.
Therefore, I say unto you, What things soever ye de-
sire, when ye pray, believe that ye receive them, and ye
shall have them.
And when ye stand praying, forgive, if ye have ought
against any: that your Father also which is in heaven
may forgive you your trespasses.

(Mark 11:23–25)

These verses occur right after Jesus entered the temple and begin to cast out them that sold and overthrew the tables of the moneychangers.

Even though He had spoken to the fig tree the day prior to entering the temple, Mark 11:23–25 was in response to Peter reminding the Lord Jesus about what had happened to the tree.

Jesus was not referencing the tree only; He was using the tree as an example that faith allows you to speak and it will come to pass. The mountain as this verse illustrates anything that rises up, as lifting itself as an obstacle.

Therefore, anything that rises itself above the knowledge and will of God and Christ Jesus the Lord; speak to it with faith not wavering.

Are you using the keys, the benefits God has provided through Christ described in this insight? Such that the earnest expectation of the creature is seeing the manifestation of the sons of God (Romans 8:15–19).

The number "7" represents perfection. On day seven of creation God rested from His work and created Adam a man manifesting the creator, which had a living soul capable of eternity.

Rest from your works and accept the supernatural will of God.

Do you see God's triune work and manifestation in your life? You are a new creature able to manifest the new spiritual life that has been given you. Allowing you to be perfect as our Father is perfect (Matthew 5:48).

Mark the perfect man, and behold the upright: for the end of that man is peace.

(Psalms 37:37)

For we which have believed do enter into rest, as he said, As I have sworn in my wrath, if they shall enter into my rest: although the works were finished from the foundation of the world.

(Hebrews 4:3)

It is finished, walk in it! Amen!

CONSULTATION

The number "8" represents a new beginning.

*Therefore, if any man be in Christ, he is a new crea-
ture; old things are passed away; behold, all things are
become new.*

(2 Corinthians 5:17)

You are a new creature in Christ by the creative
act of God as we progress through the process of our
spiritual transformation.

Job is the oldest written account in the Bible. We
don't know who wrote the book, but it happened after
the flood (Genesis 9:13–19).

What happened to Job was a confirmation that all
things work together for the good of those who are in
Christ Jesus (Romans 8:28). It gave Job a testimony at
the end of the vast depth of God in His dealings with
man.

This discussion relating to Job truly fits in this
section of this work for Job truly experienced regeneration and a form of resurrection from the troubles that
occurred in the beginning of the book about his life
until the new life he received at the end of the book (a
new beginning).

Job dwelt in the land of Uz (Job 1:1). The word Uz means to consult or consultation, which is to have a formal discussion about a topic. The very location of where Job lived gave us an idea of what the book of Job is about. The consultation of how God interacts in the lives of men!

Isaiah 1:18 also states, "Come let us reason together, saith the Lord: though your sins be as scarlet, they shall be as white as snow; though they be red like crimson, they shall be as wool."

This is a new beginning for you as you learn how to commune and consult with God on the issues that occur around you in your realm of influence. Whether the issue is related to a problem, direction to take, related to a weakness, or related to others around you.

Job went from despair to a new beginning; but there is great insight in the events that happened in Job's life.

Job is a written discourse between Job and three of his friends (Eliphaz, Bildad, and Zophar—Job 2:11) and then the consultation of God to Job occurred in chapters 38, 39, 40, and 41. What words for your life is God wanting to speak to you as your personal consultant?

Job and his friends debated whether the events occurring in Job's life was due to the result of sin committed by Job or his family.

In this insight, I will give what I believe the intent was for this book of the Bible.

Did the testing of Job have a distinction to be for good or for evil? The Lord God knew the answer before the testing of Job even started.

In the first two chapters we see details of conversations between God, the sons of God and Satan. God asked Satan had he considered His servant Job (Job 1:8). We know the purpose of Satan is to kill, steal, deceive, and destroy (John 10:10 and 1 Peter 5:8). And more likely than not that is what Satan was doing when he told God he had been going to and fro in the earth, and from walking up and down in it. He still does this today, but it is up to us to resist his trespasses because we have the keys to the kingdom.

Isn't it interesting that God asked Satan if he had tested Job? The response from Satan was that God had a hedge about Job, he was unable to kill, steal, deceive, or destroy anything that was related to Job.

Job gives us a great view of how God interacts in the life of men. It gives a picture of the faithfulness of God's blessings in our life as we live and give reverence to Him (Job 1:1–5).

Notice in verse 5 Job constantly was concerned with sin. He also, feared judgement that could impact the lives of his family and possessions.

Steps to Our New Beginning!

Step No. 1 is to concur your sin consciousness. If you are always concerned with sin your focus is wrong. We are delivered from sin through Christ. We must allow the Holy Ghost to work on our inner man through study of God's word. Realize you are the righteousness of God in Christ Jesus!

Job's continual concern of failure toward God gave Satan a plan of action once God removed the hedge. There was attacks on Job's family and possessions. And then finally on his health.

Job never sinned with his lips (Job 2:10), but the battle was within himself.

*For the thing which I greatly feared is come upon Me,
and that which I was afraid of is come unto me.*

(Job 3:25)

God allowed Satan to use the things that Job was
concerned about internally (in his mind, heart, and
soul) to test him. Bringing Job into a new way of life
internally and outwardly.

I like the book of Job because it dispels all cookie
cutter concepts of God. A cookie cutter concept is a
concept that puts God in a box. It illustrates that God
always responds in a certain way.

We know God will not allow His Word to be void
(of no effect). So at times we look at God as a robot.
If I do this, He'll do that. Following the concept that
our lives are always destined for blessings continually.
If there are no trials, how do we know where we are
in our spiritual walk. Jesus was even tested (Matthew
4:1–11).

God will bless us and wants to bless us, but there
is a path designed for each of us to travel. That path is
to help us understand God, know His ways, and how
He applies His will to our lives. So we must understand
the events of life are tools for our development.

Step No. 2: Be developed into His image as you
progress through your new beginning. Growth is not
always achieved when things are easy for us.

The book of Job illustrates the broadness and
depth of God as He works in our lives. Using all things
for your benefit and development.

In consultation (discussion) with Job, Bildad
asked Job, "Doth God pervert judgment or doth the Almighty pervert justice?" (Job 8:2–7).

Basically, he was saying God is a righteous judge;

therefore, God's judgment is upon you for your sins. Bildad was wrong, the events happening to Job were not a result of Job's sinfulness; but the result of God giving us a glimpse of how we are seen in God's eyes because of Christ's sacrifice (Job 1:8).

God is all powerful and all knowing. He knows what to orchestrate in our lives to benefit us spiritually and naturally, for ourselves and for others.

Did Job know the things happening to him would benefit him and others as it became written scripture to help people four thousand years later. His experience can be used to help reveal to us that sometimes we must be challenged in ways that seem not to be the will of God.

For who hath known the mind of the Lord?
Or who hath been his counsellor?
Or who hath first given to him, and it
Shall be recompensed unto him again?
For of him, and through him, and to him,
Are all things: to whom be glory forever.
Amen.

(Romans 11:34–36)

Hallelujah to God! All things work through Him; even though we can't know His mind or give Him counsel; but we can pray unto Him and He will listen!

The book of Job shows us we must consult with God to understand the present events and to get a glimpse of the future events in our lives, it shows that the purpose of God at times is beyond our understanding, but in the end if we stay faithful it will become clear. Read Job chapter 42. Job acknowledges that God can do everything He chooses and that no one's thoughts can be hidden from God (Job 42:2).

Step No. 3: is to overcome fear and doubt. Job overcame fear through this experience and the documentation of these events in the Bible are written to explain God uses all things for our benefit and development as His children.

Look at the Apostle Paul, would you think God would use a man that traveled from city to city seeking to persecute Believers in Christ and gave consent for executions by stoning?

Yet this same man's letters account for the largest portion of the New Testament writings. I'll say it once more; we can't put God in a box to say this is how it works or should work relating to events that occur in our lives. Unless God reveals it to us by the Holy Ghost, we can't always know what events are permissioned attacks of Satan for our development and which attacks are motivated by Satan to get us to yield and fall into unbelief. This is why *we must consult God* to gain understanding of the event and the proper way to respond. You can't bind something orchestrated by God for your development!

Job has taught me everything is in God's timing and His timing will be beneficial to us spiritually first and then naturally.

What seems to be delayed in your life: physical deliverance, a new job, waiting for an approval, seeking a new opportunity, or starting a ministry; they are all in God's timing as you submit unto Him. And the events that occur leading up to the breakthrough could seem troubling, but you must seek God and behold the day of your liberation.

Remember Insight No. 3 God walked through the garden seeking Adam and in Insight No. 5 when Elijah was in the cave a still small voice spoke to him.

During times of indecision in your life God is there waiting to consult with you to show you your new beginning.

Look at Abraham (at the age of one hundred) and Sarah (at the age of ninety) never having children. Do you think they wondered about this? God promised Abraham the lineage of God's people would come through him.

In verse 10 and 14 of Genesis chapter 18 there was a phrase used, "according to the time of life" relating to the birth of a child that would be the seed for God's people.

The word time, in this verse means a period of time, an appointed time, or season. Abraham and Sarah had not conceived a child all those years because there was an appointed time for Isaac to be born.

Your season and new beginning are now!

Step No. 4: is continuing to work out your salvation and relationship with God. All the cares of life you are seeking after have an appointed time to be conceived, if you stay true to God. He will orchestrate the events; they may not be exactly how you saw it but they will be what's best.

Oh, Lord, help us to understand the timing you have set for our lives and the paths for us to dwell in. Help us to hear you speak in every instance of concern in our lives!

Are you in a season where you just don't know why things are happening or the reason for them happening?

Is there fear and doubt working within you?

Seek God and He will reveal the answer and be a deliverer, whatever the case may be. Receive your new beginning!

The number "8" represents a new beginning, with the capability to consulted with God? As it will be in the one-thousand-year reign with Christ (Revelation 20:1–3).

After Job's consultation with God and he showed humility by praying for the friend that accused him; God gave him a new beginning and double for his trouble (Job 42:10).

INSIGHT #9

NINTH-HOUR EXPERIENCE

The number "9" shows completeness and finality.

This insight is meant to give testimony of experiences documented in the Bible that your faith and confidence will expand as Jesus mentioned in Mark 11:23 about removing the mountains in your life.

Your life has the opportunity for the miraculous! As demonstrated in the book of Acts. Are there acts orchestrated by God occurring in your life.

Read Matthew 27:46–54:

And about the ninth hour Jesus cried with a loud voice, saying, Eli, Eli, lama sabachthani? That is to say, My God, my God, why hast thou forsaken me?

(Matthew 27:46)

And, behold, the veil of the temple was rent in twain from the top to the bottom; and the earth did quake, and the rocks rent.

(Matthew 27:51)

The death of Jesus on the cross allowed the ability for all men to access God in the Holy of Holies in the temple of God; as signified by the veil being rent.

Read Acts 3:1–9:

Then Peter said, Silver and gold have I none; but such as I have give I thee; in the name of Jesus Christ of Nazareth rise up and walk.

(Acts 3:6)

The ninth hour was the time of prayer. The man at the gate called Beautiful was asking for alms, but Peter through the power instilled by Christ gave him much more.

Horaios is the Greek word for beautiful meaning belonging to the right hour or season; produced at the right time. (15) This is telling us that there are miraculous events that will be produced at the right time, at the right moment during the right season. Remember Insight No. 8 the season for Abraham and Sarah to conceive Isaac.

Glory to His Holy Name! Are you entering a miraculous period in God's timing?

Read Acts 10:1–45:

And when Cornelious look on the angel, he was afraid, and said, What is it, Lord? And he said unto him, Thy prayers and thine alms are come up for a memorial before God.

(Acts 10:4)

While Peter yet spake these words, the Holy Ghost fell on all them which heard the word.

(Acts 10:44)

God communicated to Cornelious in a vision at the ninth hour during prayer (verse 3); he also communicated to Peter at the sixth hour the next day in a vision concerning God's choice to bring gentiles into the family of God for Cornelious was a gentile sending to bring Peter to his home. God is no respecter of person. The gifts of God are available to all if they choose to walk in His presence as Cornelious did.

Notice fasting and prayer was occurring or about to occur during these first two events of the miraculous power of God being displayed.

Read Acts 12:6–16:

And, behold, the angel of the Lord came upon him, and a light shined in the prison: and he smote Peter on the side, and raised him up, saying, Arise up quickly. And his chains fell off from his hands.

(Acts 12:7)

God will send his ministering spirits to make a way for you. In verse 12 the brethren had gathered at Mary's house the mother of John to pray and Peter knocked on the door after his deliverance.

Seek and you will find, knock and it shall be opened.

Read John 11:33–44.

Jesus lifted up his eyes, and said, Father, I thank thee that thou hast heard me.

(John 11:41)

And I knew that thou hearest me always: but because of the people which stand by I said it, that they may believe that thou hast sent me.
He cried with a loud voice, Lazarus, come forth.

(John 11:42–43)

Jesus had already asked God to raise up Lazarus,

before He got to the point of executing the task. We should follow the same example; pray and ask ahead of time.

Jesus groaned in spirit and wept because He was troubled at their inability to connect what he was about to do; because of their unbelief. This was a setup, Jesus waited on purpose to let Lazarus die.

God has also called you forth from death to life and you have been loosed. Raised a new by the supernatural work of Christ (John 11:44).

You are of God, little children, and have overcome them: because greater is he that is in you, than he that is in the world.

(1 John 4:4)

We can demonstrate this enlightenment, an awakening filled with inspiration, the finality of man engaging in the work of God.

Finally, my brethren, be strong in the Lord, and in the power of his might.

(Ephesians 6:10)

The number "9" represents completeness and finality. When the one-thousand-year reign of Christ is over on this earth then shall the new heaven and earth appear with the New Jerusalem (Revelation 21:1–2).

Are you in a place of preparation to experience 9th hour events, before the return of Christ?

THE FEW

The number "10" testifies of responsibility to the order of God.

Therefore, all things whatsoever ye would that men should do to you, do ye even so to them: for this is the law and the prophets.
Enter ye in at the strait gate: for wide is the gate, and broad is the way, that leadeth to destruction, and many there be which go in thereat:
Because strait is the gate, and narrow is the way, which leadeth unto life, and few there be that find it.

(Matthew 7:12–14)

It isn't the many who finds the complete and perfect ways of God or understands the order of things to achieve completeness in Him.

The earth is the Lord's, and the fulness thereof; the world, and they that dwell therein.
For he hath founded it upon the seas, and established it upon the floods.
Who shall ascend into the hill of the Lord? Or who shall stand in his holy place?
He that hath clean hands, and a pure heart; who hath

not lifted up his soul unto vanity, nor sworn deceitfully.
He shall receive the blessing from the Lord, and righ-
teousness from the God of his salvation.
This is the generation of them that seek him, that seek
thy face, O Jacob. Selah
Lift up your heads, O ye gates; and be ye lift up, ye
everlasting doors; and the King of glory shall come in.
Who is the King of glory? The Lord strong and mighty,
the Lord mighty in battle.
Lift up your heads, O ye gates; even lift them up, ye
everlasting doors; and the King of glory shall come in.
Who is the King of glory? The Lord of hosts, He is the
King of glory. Selah.

(Psalms 24)

Selah is to pause and meditate.

The gate is an enclosing structure; an opening through which people can pass through to an enclosed area (like a door frame). Doors are openings or entrance ways.

So this verse is telling us to pause and think about the Lord and allow Him in.

Into what? The enclosing structure, the frame work around our mental and spiritual state. The enclosed area of our being.

Let the Lord walk through the door into the inner most parts of your being. Many of us has not been able to submit ourselves to allow Him in completely.

Read Matthew 25:1–13.

Then shall the kingdom of heaven be likened unto ten
virgins, which took their lamps, and went forth to meet
the bridegroom.
And five of them were wise, and five were foolish.

They that were foolish took their lamps, and took no
oil with them:
But the wise took oil in their vessels with their lamps.
(Matthew 25:1–4)

These verses illustrate the need to be ready for the coming of Christ. Oil is a symbol of the Holy Ghost and lamps in those days had small storage areas for the oil, so it was necessary to replenish the lamps with oil frequently from the larger storage vessels.

In Matthew 25:12 Christ (the bridegroom) told the foolish five virgins when they returned with oil that He knew them not.

This is a perfect picture of the need for us to be in a constant process of rejuvenation by the Holy Ghost.

But after that the kindness and love of God our Saviour
toward man appeared,
Not by works of righteousness which we have done, but
according to his mercy he saved us, by the washing of
regeneration, and renewing of the Holy Ghost.
(Titus 3:4–5)

Verse 5 tells us that we are washed baptized into a new birth; a spiritual renovation; our genesis that is forming us through the revival of the Holy Ghost power in our life. This is *the continual operation of the indwelling of the Spirit of God*, which places us into a new spiritual foundation.

This is why in the parable the bridegroom told the virgins that had not refilled their lambs with oil (the Holy Ghost) he didn't know them.

An example of this is the two fillings of the Holy Ghost that occurred in the book of Acts for the disciples. Acts 2:4 the initial filling on the day of Pentecost and in Acts 4:31 a refilling after Peter and John was threatened for the healing of the man by the gate Beautiful.

And when they had prayed, the place was shaken where they were assembled together; and they were all filled with the Holy Ghost, and they spoke the word of God with boldness.

(Acts 4:31)

We should have one encounter after another with the Holy Ghost during our life time. If we don't stay refreshed by the spirit, we could become as water does that stands still. It becomes infested with bacteria and disease not fit for the drinking; a symbol of us being unfit and left behind as the five unwise virgins were.

This reminds me of scripture in Matthew 7:21, when Christ spoke on the kingdom of heaven and said, "not everyone that saith unto me Lord, Lord shall enter into the kingdom of heaven."

He then said, they gave Him their resume: I prophesied in thy name, and cast out devils, and many wonderful works have I done in your name (Matthew 7:22).

Christ said, "I never knew you; depart ye worker of iniquity."

Remember the gifts of God are without repentance (Romans 11:29). Once a gift is given, God doesn't take it back, even if we misuse what he has given.

Those who are in relationship with the Father through Jesus Christ with the renewing of the Holy Ghost are His.

Remember in 2 Thessalonians 2:9; Paul said,

"Christ is coming after the working of Satan with power signs and lying wonders." Demonstration of wonders don't mean you know God.

The number "10" testifies of responsibility to the order of God. After the New Jerusalem appears, all men will live by the order of God for He, Himself shall dwell with us (Revelation 21:3).

Are you demonstrating the complete and perfect work of Christ in your life? Do you have the fruits of the Spirit? (Galatians 5:22–24).

God will dwell with you now if you ask Him.

EPILOGUE

My desire for this work is to help Believers rationalize the insights discussed; enabling each insight to provide details to help the spiritual development of the reader. Solidifying your linkage to God (the Father, the Son, and the Holy Spirit), which allows our successful journey of being transformed into a new creature; as we submit every thought and action to His will as we learn to hear His guiding voice.

Your faithfulness will be documented in heaven as we operate in the gifts of the kingdom of God, through understanding, what has been provided through Christ, gaining patience and experience, then after each experience, hope is created as we strive for completeness and perfection.

APPENDIX

All scripture references were taken from The Holy Bible: King James Version, Holman Bible Publishing, Nashville, Tennessee, 1996

Dedication: Born of Water and the Spirit
    Ecclesiastes 8:5
    John 3:5–7
    John 14:16–17
    Introduction
    John 14:26
    Daniel 2:20–21
    Matthew 7:7
    Proverbs 2:3–9
    Galatians 5:22–23
    Ephesians 5:9–10
Prologue
    Romans 11:29
    Matthew 4:1–2
    Romans 12:4–7
    Jeremiah 6:16
    1 Corinthians 12:4–11
    Romans 8:19
Originated in God
    Romans 8:21

Jeremiah 1:5
1 Corinthians 15:21–22
Psalms 90:1–2
1 Corinthians 15:45–47
John 14:10
2 Corinthians 5:17–19
John 14:16–17
1 Corinthians13:12
John 14:20
Romans 1:17
Colossians 1:16
Romans 5:1–4
Matthew 10:28
Jeremiah 29:11–14
Romans 12:1–2
John 14:2–4
Hebrews 4:6–11
John 14:6–7
Genesis 1:1
The Journey
    Psalms 24:6
    Isaiah 5:20–21
    Ephesians 2:5–7
    James 1:7–8
    Ephesians 1:3–5
    Romans 7:18–25
    Exodus 33:15–18
    1 John 2:14–17
    John 10:10
Response to Temptation and Tests: Heaven and Earth
    1 Corinthians 10:13–14
    Ephesians 1:17–21
    Ephesians 2:2–3
    Hebrews 6:1

Hosea 4:61
John 5:7–8
Job 1:20–21
Revelation 20:12
Genesis 3:24
1 Corinthians 3:13
Hebrews 4:12
1 Peter 1:7
Hebrews 3:7–8
Hebrews 11:1
James 1:2–4
Matthew 6:7–8
2 Timothy 2:15
1 John 5:10–11
Hebrews 1:14
John 14:26
John 15:26
Listen
    1 John 5:8
    1 John 1:1–4
    1 John 5:4–6
    1 Timothy 4:1–2
    Ephesians 4:21–24
    Romans 10:17
    Romans 12:2
    John 1:1–4
    Matthew 6:9–10
    John 1:12
    1 Chronicles 4:10
    2 Thessalonians 2:13
    Proverbs 2:3–9
    Romans 10:8–10
    Isaiah 65:24
Keys to the Kingdom

Colossians 2:9–10
Matthew 16:19
Hebrews 1:3
Matthew 11:12
Luke 3:21–22
2 Thessalonians 2:3–8
2 Corinthians 3:18
2 Corinthians 10:4–5
Ephesians 2:6–7
Ephesians 6:10–18
Ephesians 3:20
Mark 11:23–25
Romans 8:29
Hebrews 4:3
Hebrews 11:1
2 Thessalonians 2:13
Consultation
1 John 2:20
2 Corinthians 5:17
1 John 2:27
Isaiah 1:18
Hebrews 4:12
Job 3:25
Romans 11:34–36
Ninth-Hour Experience: The Few
Matthew 27:46
Matthew 7:12–14
Matthew 27:51
Psalms 24
Acts 3:6
Matthew 25:1–4
Acts 10:4
Titus 3:4–5
Acts 10:44

Acts 4:31
Acts 12:7
John 11:41
John 11:42–43
1 John 4:4
Ephesians 6:10

ENDNOTES

1. James Strong, LLD, STD, The New Strong's Expanded Exhaustive Concordance of the Bible (Red Letter Edition), Nashville, TN: Thomas Nelson Publishers, 2010. Hebrew and Aramaic Dictionary, reference number 6440.

2. James Strong, Hebrew and Aramaic Dictionary, reference number 6441.

3. James Strong, Hebrew and Aramaic Dictionary, reference number 5117.

4. James Strong, LLD, STD, The New Strong's Expanded Exhaustive Concordance of the Bible (Red Letter Edition), Nashville, TN: Thomas Nelson Publishers, 2010. Greek Dictionary of the New Testament, reference number 2937.

5. James Strong, Greek Dictionary of the New Testament, reference number 3986.

6. James Strong, Greek Dictionary of the New Testament, reference number 189.

7. James Strong, Greek Dictionary of the New Testament, reference number 3056.

8. James Strong, Greek Dictionary of the New Testament, reference number 1411.

9. James Strong, Greek Dictionary of the New Testament, reference number 5287.

10. James Strong, Greek Dictionary of the New Testament, reference number 1650.

11. James Strong, Greek Dictionary of the New Testament, reference number 2807.

12. James Strong, Greek Dictionary of the New Testament, reference number 932.

13. James Strong, Greek Dictionary of the New Testament, reference number 1210.

14. James Strong, Greek Dictionary of the New Testament, reference number 3089.

15. James Strong, Greek Dictionary of the New Testament, reference number 5611.

BIBLIOGRAPHY

Holman Bible Publishing, Giant Print Reference Bible (King James Version), Nashville, Tennessee, 1996.
James Strong, LLD, STD, The New Strong's Expanded Exhaustive Concordance of the Bible (Red Letter Edition), Nashville, TN: Thomas Nelson Publishers, 2010.

About the Author

The author has enjoyed thirty-nine years as a child of the King.

He completed the requirement to receive a Master of Arts degree in biblical studies in May of 2005.

While ministering for congregations in Oklahoma, Texas, Missouri, and Louisiana; he self-published two other Christian focused publications.

The goal of this third work is to help the Believer be aware that the time is now to equip themselves to become overcomers.

For whatsoever is born of God overcometh the world: and this is the victory that overcomeeth the world, even our faith.
Who is he that overcometh the world, but he that believeth that Jesus is the Son of God?

(1 John 5:4–5)

Thy kingdom come; Thy will be done in earth, as it is in heaven.

(Matthew 6:10)

```
    W
  H I S
    L
    L
```